the adopter's handbook

information
resources
services

Amy Neil Salter

Updated by Jenifer Lord

BAAF
ADOPTION
& FOSTERING

Published by
British Association for Adoption & Fostering
(BAAF)
Saffron House
6–10 Kirby Street
London EC1N 8TS
www.baaf.org.uk

Charity registration 275689 (England and Wales) and SC039337
(Scotland)

© Amy Neil Salter, 2002, 2004, 2006, 2012
New edition 2013

British Library Cataloguing in Publication Data
A catalogue record for this book is available from the British Library

ISBN 978 1 907585 89 0

Project management by Shaila Shah, Director of Publications, BAAF

Designed by Helen Joubert Design

Printed in Great Britain by The Lavenham Press

Trade distribution by Turnaround Publisher Services, Unit 3, Olympia
Trading Estate, Coburg Road, London N22 6TZ

BAAF is the leading UK-wide membership organisation for all those
concerned with adoption, fostering and child care issues.

Contents

Acknowledgements

Several people have helped make this guide what it is. Useful information has been supplied and sections and draft of the guide have been reviewed by many professionals and experienced parents involved in adoption. I am grateful for their input, advice and guidance. Thanks to members of Adoption UK, who completed the initial questionnaire which sparked this process, and to the following people for their comments on parts or all of the original draft: Hedi Argent, Daphne Batty, Miranda Davies, Lynda Gilbert, Gill Haworth, Marion Hundleby, Mary Lane, Jenifer Lord, Philly Morrall, Shaila Shah, John Simmonds and Justin Simon. Katrina Wilson and Florence Merredew supplied helpful information for the second edition.

About the author

Amy Neil Salter has had a personal involvement with adoption and is a freelance medical writer by profession. She is currently a practising psychotherapist at a community mental health centre in the USA.

This book is dedicated to her parents, who taught her everything.

This edition

This edition was updated by Jenifer Lord who was for many years a Child Placement consultant in BAAF's Southern region. She is a member of an adoption and permanence panel and has written several books on adoption for BAAF.

Is adoption right for you?

'... it will be important for all concerned to be realistic in recognising that long-term and persistent trauma can result in behaviours that are both challenging to live with and resistant to change.'
S. Byrne, *Linking and Introductions*, BAAF, 2000

Clearly, there are many children who need a loving and secure home, and many more people are needed to be adoptive parents. But this doesn't *necessarily* mean adoption is the right choice for everyone. It is important to consider in a clear and logical manner your decision to adopt – to avoid the temptation to be led to your decision purely by emotion.

The fact that you are reading this guide means you are investigating the option of adopting children. You and your family may have discussed many of the different issues involved already. But if you don't know much about adoption, or don't know anyone who has adopted children, you might want to think about some of the following questions.

Why do I/we want to adopt?

We cannot escape the fact that deciding to have children, through birth or through adoption, fulfils some of our own needs and desires to become parents and to raise a family. After all, this is a natural process in life. Yet most children waiting for adoption have specific emotional and physical needs (see Section 4 for more explanation) and require parents who can commit to being with them through good times and through tough times. The process of adoption, therefore, must necessarily focus on the *child's* needs and on meeting those needs as much as possible.

When you begin the process of adoption, you must also be willing to address your own emotional needs (for example, attachment issues from your own childhood, infertility issues, grief over a lost child, etc.) and must be sure that adoption is not simply a route to overcome your own difficulties.

Is parenting an adopted child different from parenting my own birth child?

Yes. Most children who are placed for adoption have experienced some degree of abuse and/or neglect. And all children needing adoption suffer the trauma of separation from, and loss of, their birth family. These events affect children of *all* ages (even infants) and in many different ways (see Section 4 for more information about these effects). While most children are able to "recover" from their experiences when placed in a loving environment, it is important to understand that the road to recovery can be difficult and frustrating for both the child and the adoptive parents.

It is also important to understand that older children (age 3+), especially, will have begun to develop their own personality and habits by the time they are adopted. As parents, your personality and habits will still influence the child, but less so than if the child had been born to you.

Is it "easier" to parent an older child or a younger child?

Research* has shown that infant adoptions are generally successful for both the child and the parents. Yet, there is no guarantee that a younger child will have fewer difficulties than an older child. Even babies can suffer the effects of early trauma or neglect (see Section 4). Only you can decide what age child you want to adopt. The most important consideration is to determine how you can best meet the needs of that child.

Can children who have experienced trauma, abuse and/or neglect ever overcome these experiences?

Yes. Section 4 of this guide describes the many complex emotional, developmental and physical difficulties children can experience as a result of abuse and/or neglect. In some cases, such experiences can affect the physical growth and development of neural connections in the brain and thus affect the child's emotions and behaviour. Studies† have shown that, with appropriate treatment (medical, psychiatric and/or psychological), these neural connections can form – the brain can be helped to adapt to compensate for earlier neglect.

When considering adoption, the two key things to remember are:

- providing a loving and secure home will help the child, but may not help the child resolve *all* of his or her problems – you may have to seek additional assistance from a variety of sources; and

- the wounds of abuse and neglect run deep – even if the child was removed from the abusive environment at an early age.

As adoptive parents, therefore, we must look realistically at our own expectations of our child and his or her "recovery". It may take many years (perhaps a lifetime) for the child to overcome the complex effects of early trauma.

How does the adoption process work?

Getting started

You can get useful general information from First4Adoption, a national information service on adoption in England (www.first4adoption.co.uk)

---

* C. Sellick, J. Thoburn, T. Philpot, *What works in adoption and foster care?*, Barnardo's/BAAF, 2004

† J. Selwyn, W. Sturgess, D. Quinton and C. Baxter, *Costs and Outcomes of Non-Infant Adoptions*, BAAF, 2006; B. Perry, *Maltreated Children: Experience, brain development and the next generation*, W.W. Norton, New York, 1995

HELPFUL BOOKS

For more information and publications about the effects of early trauma, see Section 4 and Appendix 1 of this guide.

Attachment, Trauma and Resilience: Therapeutic caring for children
by Kate Cairns, BAAF, 2002
Written by someone who fostered several children over a 25-year period, this book provides an illustration of family life with children who had lived through overwhelming stress and how they were helped to overcome it.

First Steps in Parenting the Child Who Hurts: Tiddlers and toddlers by
Caroline Archer, Jessica Kingsley, 1999
This book approaches the attachment and developmental issues that arise when even the youngest child is in your care.

Next Steps in Parenting the Child Who Hurts: Tykes and teens by
Caroline Archer, Jessica Kingsley, 1999
This book follows on logically from the *First Steps* book and continues into the challenging journey through childhood and into adolescence.

The Primal Wound: Understanding the adopted child by Nancy Verrier,
BAAF, 2009 (UK edn)
This book contains profound insights and revelations on what being adopted means to adopted people. The book explores the "primal wound" that results when a child is separated from his or her mother and the trauma it can cause.

Coming Home to Self: Healing the primal wound by Nancy Verrier,
BAAF, 2010 (UK edn)
Considers the effects of separation trauma on brain development and explores some of the most troubling emotions and examines ways of healing and achieving meaningful relationships and personal power.

Loving and Living with Traumatised Children by Megan Hirst, BAAF,
2005
Looks at the experience of adopting traumatised children and the effects this can have on their carers and adoptive parents, based on the experiences of nine individuals.

or from the British Association for Adoption and Fostering (BAAF) (www.baaf.org.uk) or from Adoption UK – a UK-wide self-help organisation for adoptive and prospective adoptive parents (www.adoptionuk.org).

Once you have decided you are interested in adopting a child, the first step is to contact a local authority's adoption team or a voluntary adoption agency to ask for information and procedures. These usually cover geographical areas and are all listed on the First4Adoption and BAAF websites, as well as in *Adopting a Child* (Lord, 2013).

If you are interested in adopting a specific child you have seen in a family-finding publication or website: you should contact the organisation that produces the publication/website for information and then the local authority looking after the child.

When you contact an adoption agency: you will receive written information and you will be offered a follow-up interview with a social worker and/or an invitation to an information meeting, or a pre-planned phone call. This will give you the opportunity to find out more about adoption and about the waiting children, to ask questions and to talk a bit about your hopes and plans. This should happen within 10 days of your initial enquiry to the agency. If, after this, you decide to proceed, you will need to formally register your interest in doing so. The agency will provide you with a Registration of Interest form with which to do this.

The key players

There are five key players in the adoption process:

- the child;
- the local authority adoption team OR the voluntary adoption agency which has assessed you, your assessing social worker and team manager;
- the local authority which is responsible for the child (which may or may not be the same one as above), the child's social worker and team manager;
- you, the prospective adoptive parent/s; and
- the birth parent(s) or child's legal guardians.

The courts also play a role in the adoption process, at different points along the way.

Voluntary adoption agencies

Voluntary adoption agencies are usually smaller agencies than local authorities. They work to the same regulations, guidance and national minimum standards as local authorities. They recruit, assess, approve and support adoptive parents who will have children looked after by a local authority placed with them.

Social workers

All social workers in the UK are required to have a qualification approved by the Health and Care Professions Council (HCPC) or equivalent body. They are required to be registered with these bodies. The qualification involves a minimum of three years' training, culminating in a degree.

The following organisations are involved in the development and management of the social care industry:

- **Health and Care Professions Council** (HCPC)

- **Ofsted** (Office for Standards in Education, Children's Services and Skills)

- **Department for Education** (DfE)

- **Social Care Institute for Excellence** (SCIE) collects and synthesises up-to-date knowledge about what works in social care and makes that widely available.

National Minimum Standards are in force to specify how adoption and fostering services should be delivered. Adoption services are inspected every three years against these Standards (see Appendix 3). The DfE publishes guidance – statutory and practice guidance – which shapes the way that adoption and fostering services are provided.

Figure 2 shows a *general* flowchart of the route to adoption of a child, as seen by the local authority. Below, we look in detail at the adoption process for prospective adopters.

How can I prepare for adoption?

No one can ever be fully "prepared" for the adoption process and for the eventual arrival of a child in their home. But there are things you can do to make the process a bit easier and to "initially" prepare yourself as much as possible to meet the needs of the child who may become a part of your family.

- Once you tell an agency about your interest in adoption, you will be given written and verbal information. When you have applied to the agency you will be given preparation, which may be by attendance at groups. You will have a chance to explore a range of issues about adoption and children's needs. You can read *Preparing to Adopt* (the Workbook), part of a training guide published by BAAF in 2010 (to be updated in 2013) and watch the DVD that accompanies it (Appendix 1).

- You can access the e-learning material on the First4Adoption website – www.first4adoption.org.uk.

- You can read about the adoption process, so you understand the functions and responsibilities of everyone involved – this helps avoid misunderstandings. *Adopting a Child*, a popular guide published by BAAF and regularly revised (most recently in autumn 2013), provides a comprehensive account.

- You can gain experience of other people's children, e.g. attend Parentcraft classes at your local clinic or hospital, or volunteer to help at your local school, play group or nursery.

- You can meet adoptive parents, through joining Adoption UK.

Figure 2 **Process for identifying a family after a decision that a child should be placed for adoption**

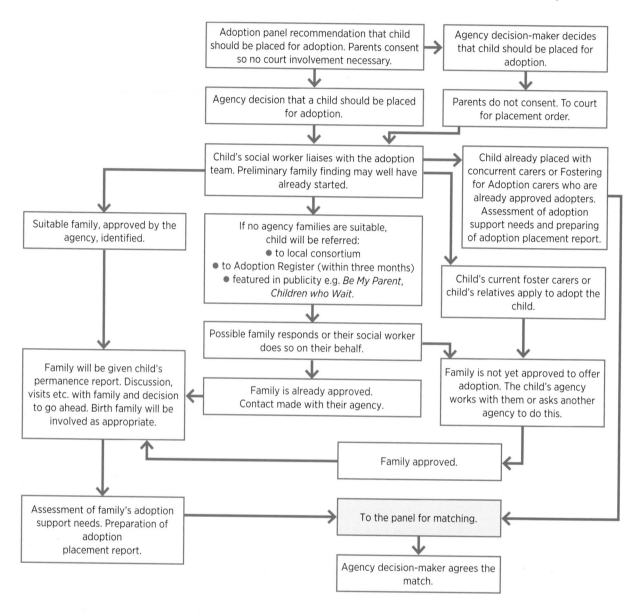

Reproduced (with amendments) from *Effective Adoption Panels,* 6th edn., BAAF, 2013.

- If you are a lesbian or gay adopter, you can meet others through joining New Family Social.

- You can read about and be aware of the impact of trauma and neglect on children of all ages.

- You can read about the experiences of others who have adopted (see booklist).

- You can read about adoption law from the perspective of adopters in *Adoption Law for Adopters,* published by Adoption UK in January 2006.

It is impossible to prepare yourself for every aspect of the adoption process, because you can't anticipate everything that may occur. The best preparation is to read about the adoption process and about the children as you go along, so you will know how to access help right away, if you need it.

HELPFUL ORGANISATIONS

General information about adoption

Adoption UK
A UK-wide support organisation for adoptive parents and prospective adopters with local groups and messageboards. Also publishes a monthly magazine, *Adoption Today*, with news, views and features, and a supplement and website, *Children Who Wait*, which features children needing adoption.

Linden House, 55 The Green, South Bar Street, Banbury, Oxfordshire OX16 9AB
Helpline: 0844 848 7900
Tel: 01295 752240
Email: admin@adoptionuk.org.uk
www.adoptionuk.org.uk

British Association for Adoption & Fostering (BAAF)
Has offices throughout the UK and provides up-to-date information about all aspects of adoption, including information about adoption agencies and answers to general questions about adoption. Also publishes useful pamphlets and guides including *Adopting a Child*, and runs a family-finding service, *Be My Parent*, which features waiting children, both in print and online. Also manages the Adoption Register for England and Wales, Scotland's Adoption Register, and the Adoption Regional Information System in Northern Ireland, for these countries' respective governments.

Saffron House, 6–10 Kirby Street, London EC1N 8TS
Tel: 020 7421 2600
www.baaf.org.uk
www.bemyparent.org.uk

Department for Education
The government department responsible for adoption and fostering services and for other services to children and families.

Tel: 0370 000 2288
www.education.gov.uk/ childrenandyoungpeople/families/ adoption

New Family Social is a UK charity for lesbian, gay, bisexual and transgender adopters, foster carers and their children. It provides advice and information, a vibrant messageboard, as well as social events for parents and children to get together.

PO Box 66244
London E9 9BD
Tel: 0843 289 9457
www.newfamilysocial.org.uk

First4Adoption is a new dedicated information service for people interested in adopting a child from England. Information line open 10am–6pm Monday–Friday.

Tel: 0300 222 0022
Email: helpdesk@first4adoption.org.uk
www.first4adoption.org.uk

Who can adopt?

Almost anyone can apply to be an adoptive parent if they can show that they can provide a loving, secure home that will meet the needs of a particular child.

Adoption Guidance makes clear that no one can be denied the opportunity to be considered as an adoptive parent because of ethnic background, marital status, sexuality or age. It spells out the eligibility criteria:

- The prospective adopter(s) is single, married, in a civil partnership or an unmarried couple (same sex or opposite sex) and 21 years old. (The birth parent in a step-parent adoption must be 18 or older.)

- The prospective adopter or one of them has their permanent home (domicile) in England, Wales, Scotland, Northern Ireland, the Channel Islands, on the Isle of Man, or both members of a couple have been habitually resident there for at least a year before they apply to court for an adoption order.

- Neither prospective adopter nor an adult member of their household has been convicted or cautioned for a specified offence. These are principally offences against children.

What sorts of families can adopt?

Although the majority of adopters are married couples, all sorts of families can and do adopt very successfully. In fact, research* has found that some family structures, such as single parents, can better meet the needs of particular children (such as those who have been sexually abused or who may need to interact with only one parent).

Couples who live together, as well as married or civil registered couples, can adopt jointly.

We should keep in mind that children may have fewer predetermined views about families.

Here are some answers to common questions prospective adopters ask.

We are foster carers and we want to adopt our foster child. How do we do this? If you have fostered a child for at least one year, or longer, you can apply to the court for an adoption order, whether or not the child's local authority agrees. However, you must give notice in writing to the local authority three months before you make the application. If the local authority does not agree with your application, you will only be eligible for limited post-adoption support. You can apply much sooner with the

---

*See M. Owen, *Novices, Old Hands and Professionals: Adoption by single people*, BAAF, 1999 and L. Mellish *et al*, *Gay, Lesbian and Heterosexual Adoptive Families*, BAAF, 2013.

HELPFUL BOOKS

One of the Famiily: A handbook for kinship carers, by Hedi Argent, BAAF, 2005
A practical handbook which gives family and friends who may become kinship carers information about the choices they can make, the child care system and the support they can expect.

Becoming Dads by Pablo Fernández, BAAF, 2011
A diarised narrative account of how Pablo and Mike adopt their son.

Flying Solo by Julia Wise, BAAF, 2007
A single parent's adoption story.

Is it True you have Two Mums? by Ruby Clay, BAAF, 2011
Charts the adoption journey of a lesbian couple who adopt three girls.

Looking After our Own: The stories of black and Asian adopters edited by Hope Massiah, BAAF, 2005
Stories from a number of black and Asian adopters about their adoption experiences.

Loving and Living with Traumatised Children: Reflections by adoptive parents by Megan Hirst, BAAF, 2005
A group of adopters tell of their experiences and the effect on themselves of adopting traumatised children.

Novices, Old Hands and Professionals: Adoption by single people by Morag Owen, BAAF, 1999
Documents and comments on the experiences of single adopters and their children.

The Pink Guide to Adoption for Lesbians and Gay Men (second edition) by Nicola Hill, BAAF, 2012
A step-by-step guide to adopting, including accounts by those going through the process.

agreement of the local authority and it is best to discuss your wishes with them and, if possible, to go through the adoption process with them. There is a "fast track" for approved foster carers in England who wish to adopt. They can enter the process at Stage Two, which provides for an assessment and decision within four months.

We want to adopt our grandchildren. How can we do this? As relatives of the children, whether or not they are looked after by the local authority, you can apply to adopt them after the children have lived with you for three years. You can apply to the court for permission to apply sooner than this. You must give written notice to the local authority at least three months before you apply for the adoption order. The court will decide if the adoption order or any other order, such as a residence order or a special guardianship order, is in the children's best interests. The court will take into account the local authority's views about this. If the children are

Figure 3 **Families offering placements – from first enquiry to approval**

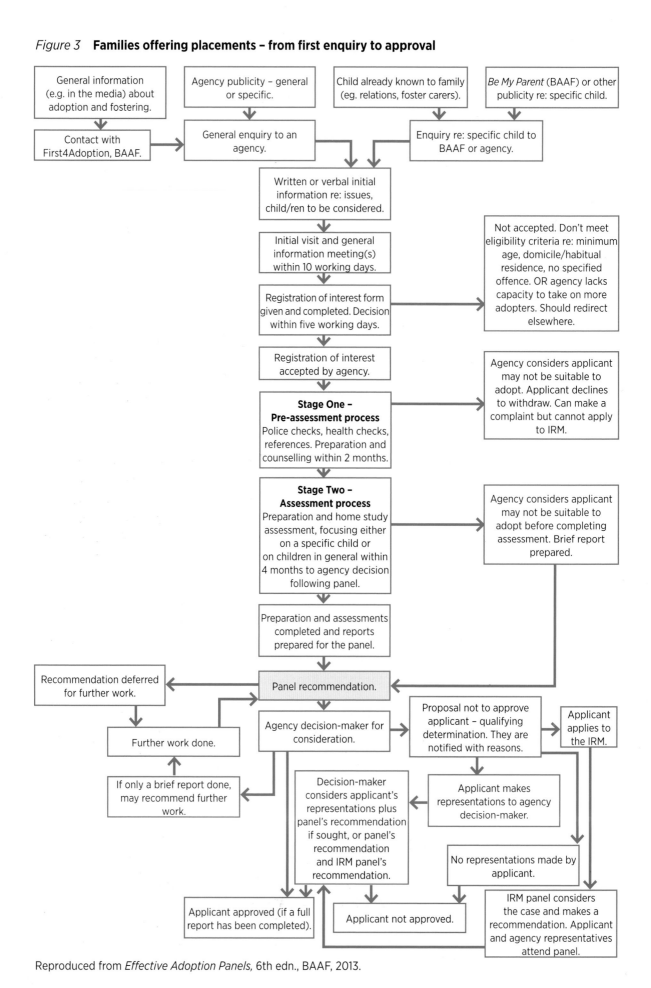

Reproduced from *Effective Adoption Panels,* 6th edn., BAAF, 2013.

looked after by the local authority and you are currently fostering them, the answer above in relation to foster carers applies to you.

My husband and I are from different ethnic backgrounds. Will this affect our ability to adopt a child? In fact, there are many children of mixed ethnic backgrounds, so families such as yours are particularly needed.

My partner and I are not married, but we want to adopt a child. Can we do this? Yes. Unmarried couples (lesbian, gay, or heterosexual) or couples who have not entered into a civil partnership, can adopt jointly.

My partner and I are in a same-sex relationship. Can we adopt a child? Yes. Lesbian or gay couples can adopt jointly just as any other couple.

I am a single parent. Can I adopt a child? Yes, single people can adopt. Research has found that some children benefit from placement with a single adult; for example, girls who have been sexually abused, and children who have witnessed severe conflict between parents or those who will benefit from the one-to-one attention and care provided by one adult.

I am in my late 40s and my partner is over 50. Can we adopt? Yes, this could be possible. Adoption Guidance states that older and more experienced adopters could have something special to offer to older children if they enjoy sufficient health and vigour to meet the child's varied demands; it cautions that too large an age gap between adopter and child may have an adverse effect upon the child. Adopters need to be able to meet the many and varied demands of children in their growing years and be there for them into adulthood.

If we had a placement that disrupted, can we apply for adoption again? If you have previously had a child placed with you for adoption and the placement did not work out for you, don't be put off. The adoption agency which originally approved you must undertake a review of your approval. They must ask their panel to make a recommendation about your continued approval, if the agency is of the view that your approval should be terminated. If the agency proposal is to terminate your approval, you can apply to the Independent Review Mechanism (IRM) for a review of that proposal.

What is concurrent planning?

This is the term given to schemes run by some agencies in which children, usually babies or toddlers, for whom there is a chance that they might return home to their birth family, are placed with families who will foster them with this aim. However, the foster carers are also approved as adopters and will adopt the child should the planned return to the birth family not be successful. In this way, the moves that a child may otherwise have to make are minimised. These schemes have to be run with the agreement and co-operation of the local courts and to tight timescales. Families who have children placed under a concurrency scheme have to be prepared to facilitate very regular contact for the child with their birth family and to be prepared that the child may return home. However, adoption often becomes the plan for these children and the carers can then adopt a child who has been placed with them from a young age. If you might be interested in becoming a carer in a concurrency scheme, First4Adoption or BAAF will be able to tell you which agencies operate such schemes.

What is Fostering for Adoption (FFA)?

The Care Planning, Placement and Case Review and Fostering Services (Miscellaneous Amendments) Regulations 2013 (which came into force on 1 July 2013) allow an agency to give an approved adopter temporary approval as a foster carer for a named child. This enables a child to be placed as a foster child with carers without them having had a full fostering assessment or panel approval as foster carers. These will be children for whom the likelihood of eventual adoption is high. However, the child is fostered until, in most cases, work with birth parents and court involvement enables an adoption plan to be agreed and the child to be matched for adoption with these carers at panel. If you might be interested in becoming an FFA carer, you should discuss this with your agency during your assessment. The children placed in this way are likely to be quite young. However, there is a risk that, for some reason, adoption is not agreed as the plan or court involvement takes longer than anticipated.

A detailed look at the process for adopters

Ten steps to becoming an adoptive parent

After you have decided to consider adopting, the main steps of the adoption process for prospective adopters are:

1   You get general information about adoption and have a pre-planned phone call or a meeting with a social worker and/or attend an adoption information meeting. You complete a Registration of Interest form.

2   Your Registration of Interest is accepted and you move on to Stage One of the assessment process. This involves initial counselling, training

and preparation, and police checks, health checks and references are undertaken.

3   You notify the agency that you wish to move to Stage Two, which involves an assessment by a social worker of your suitability to adopt a looked after child. You will probably attend more in-depth preparation groups with other prospective adopters.

4   The report written by your social worker about you – the Prospective Adopter's Report (PAR) – is given to an adoption panel for their recommendation of your approval as prospective adopters. The agency makes the final decision.

5   If you are approved, the social workers consider a match between you and a child who has been authorised for adoption by a placement order or a section 19 parental consent. The social worker from the child's agency sends you the Child's Permanence Report and arranges to meet you to discuss the proposed match. If it is agreed that the match will proceed, the child's agency must assess your and the child's support needs and agree a support plan with you.

6   An adoption panel considers the proposed match, makes a recommendation and advises on contact, adoption support and exercise of parental responsibilities. The child's local authority then makes a decision to proceed with the match.

7   You and the child are introduced.

8   The child moves in (i.e. is placed with you).

9   An adoption order is made through the court.

10   Settling in, and post-placement and post-adoption support.

Let's look at each of these steps in detail.

1   Initial information gathering

Once you have contacted an adoption agency covering your area, they should respond within ten working days. They should invite you to an information meeting or offer you an individual visit or a pre-planned telephone call. These can take place in the evening or at a weekend if this suits you best. You will be given information on the adoption process and on the parenting needs of the children. This is an opportunity for you to consider whether adoption is likely to be right for you and how adopting a child who may have a range of complex needs will impact on your family. If you decide to proceed to the next stage, you need to complete a Registration of Interest form which the agency will supply. Among other things, this will authorise the agency to undertake the checks described in the next section. It will also confirm that you have not registered with any other agency. The agency should decide within five working days from receipt of your form whether or not to accept it. If the agency lacks the capacity to undertake assessments in the immediate future, it should advise you of this and offer to refer you to First4Adoption or to another agency.

2 Stage One – the pre-assessment process

This stage begins when the agency accepts your Registration of Interest and should normally take no more than two months to complete. The agency should discuss with you the work which will take place and should complete a written Stage One agreement with you detailing this. It should offer you some initial training and preparation and it must also complete the prescribed checks.

Checks are made of criminal records for you and members of your household aged over 18. Offences other than specified ones, i.e. those against children, need not rule you out, although the nature of the offence and how long ago it occurred will need to be carefully considered. It's vital that you are open and honest. Any attempt at deception will be taken very seriously. These checks are made to the Disclosure and Barring Service (DBS). Checks will also be made of the local authority where you live. You will be asked for the names of at least three personal referees, people who know you really well, and they will be interviewed. If you have parented children with a previous partner, the agency will want your permission to contact him or her. They may want to talk to adult children whom you've parented. They will want to check that you are not seriously in debt and that payments on your home are up to date. Finally, you will need a full medical examination carried out by your GP. This will be considered by the adoption agency's medical adviser.

If the agency decides during or at the end of Stage One that you are not suitable to adopt, it must inform you in writing with clear reasons. You may make a complaint to the agency about this or raise concerns with First4Adoption. However, you are not able to apply to the Independent Review Mechanism. You may, if you wish, take a break of up to a maximum of six months after Stage One, or you may notify the agency that you wish to proceed straight to Stage Two.

3 Stage Two – the assessment process

This stage starts when the agency receives notification from you that you wish to proceed with the assessment process. It finishes with the agency decision about your suitability as an adopter and should normally be completed within four months. A Stage Two written assessment plan must be completed with you, detailing the assessment process, dates for meetings and agreed training. The social worker designated to work with you will visit you at your home. The purpose of these visits is for the social worker to gain a detailed view of you and other family members in the home, in order to assess your suitability to adopt a child.

HELPFUL BOOKS

Adopting a Child by Jenifer Lord, BAAF, 2013
This popular guide describes what adoption means and how to go about it, including procedures and practices, legal requirements and the costs involved. It includes a list of agencies – local authority and voluntary – throughout the UK (see Appendix 1).

An Adoption Diary by Maria James, BAAF, 2006
A true story of an adoption which tracks Maria's and Rob's journey to adopting a two-year-old child, chronicling the highs and lows along the way.

Guiding you Through the Adoption Process available from Adoption UK, last revised 2009
Provides a comprehensive step-by-step guide through the adoption process.

The social worker will want to talk with your children, both those at home and usually with adult children living elsewhere. They will usually also want to meet an ex-partner with whom you have parented children. They may well want to talk further with your referees, although they will have had contact with them during Stage One of the process.

All adoption agencies are required to provide preparation and training and you will almost certainly be invited to a series of group meetings, often about six, of two to three hours each. You will be with other prospective adopters, usually about eight or ten people. As well as hearing from social workers about adoption and the children waiting, you will usually also hear from experienced adopters, an adopted adult and perhaps from a birth parent whose child has been adopted, about their experiences. You will have the opportunity to ask questions and to reflect on your own life experiences and on the impact of any adopted child on your family and how you will adapt to meet their needs.

The social worker records information on the Prospective Adopter's Report. The Prospective Adopter's Report will include a summary of the medical information about you from your GP.

Working effectively with your social worker

The goal of visits is to assess whether you are suitable to adopt and prepare you for it. Although you may feel uneasy and think the questioning and form-filling too intrusive and detailed, it is best to try to approach these visits with a relaxed, informal attitude. Open, honest communication throughout will help your social worker provide accurate information to the adoption panel. Remember that the social worker needs to ensure not only your parenting skills and capacity, and match these against a particular child or children, but also that any prospective adopter meets the legal requirements (see Section 2).

Why do adoptive parents have to be "assessed" for parenthood, when people giving birth do not? Simply because the purpose of adoption is to focus on the needs of a particular child who has had to be separated from his or her birth family – a child who is already born, with his or her own developing personality, habits and physical and emotional needs. The task of parenting a child not born to you is different and needs to be recognised as such. The social worker's role is to ensure the child's needs are matched as closely as possible to parents who can meet those needs.

YOUR RIGHTS DURING THE ASSESSMENT PROCESS

The Adoption Guidance 2013 and National Minimum Standards 2011 require that:

- Prospective adopters 'are treated fairly, without prejudice, openly and with respect. They are kept informed, on a regular basis, of the progress (or lack of progress) of their enquiry/application.' NMS 10.2

- The agency's decision about the suitability of the prospective adopter to adopt a child should be made within six months of the receipt of the Registration of Interest form. Guidance 3.24–3.52

You should be given a copy of your Prospective Adopter's Report and you are given five working days to comment upon its contents before the panel meets to consider it.

Brief report

If the agency has concerns about your suitability as a prospective adoptive parent, it should discuss these with you. However, if they are unable to be resolved it may decide to halt the process and prepare a brief report. This is presented to the adoption panel which makes a recommendation to the agency. The decision-maker in the agency can then require the agency to complete the assessment or can take the view that you are not suitable to adopt. If this is the case, you have the same rights as if the process had been completed, i.e. to make representations to the agency or to apply to the IRM – see p29.

If you have any questions or concerns which you feel unable to discuss with your social worker, or if you have particular difficulties with the assessment process or with your social worker, you should contact your social worker's manager, or the director of the adoption agency. You could also contact First4Adoption – see p15. As a very last resort, you could contact your local councillor or Member of Parliament. You may also contact:

Ofsted (Office for Standards in Education, Children's Services and Skills). It has responsibility for the reputation and inspection of all children's services. Adoption and fostering services must be inspected at least three-yearly.

Piccadilly Gate, Store Street
Manchester M1 2WD
Email: enquiries@ofsted.gov.uk
Tel: 0300 123 1231

Health and Care Professions Council, a regulatory body which sets national standards and registers people working in the health and care professions, including social workers.

Park House, 184 Kennington Park Road, London SE11 4BU
Tel: 0845 300 6184
www.hpc-uk.org

Equivalent bodies for other countries in the United Kingdom include:

- **Care Council for Wales** www.ccwales.org.uk
- **Northern Ireland Social Care Council (NISCC)** www.niscc.info
- **Scottish Social Services Council (SSSC)** www.sssc.uk.com

....

4 Your Prospective Adopter's Report (PAR) is given to an adoption panel which makes a recommendation to the agency

When your home study is completed, your social worker will submit your Prospective Adopters' Report to the local authority or voluntary agency's adoption panel. The **adoption panel** is an advisory group, established by the adoption agency or by the local authority, which:

- considers applications to be approved as adopters (either domestic or intercountry);
- recommends whether or not it believes the prospective applicant/s can meet the needs of a child and, therefore;
- recommends whether or not the applicants should be approved as adoptive parents.

The panel also makes recommendations regarding other aspects of the adoption process, such as whether a child whose parents consent should be placed for adoption and matches between children and adopters. Adoption panels can also advise about support and contact plans and the exercise of parental responsibilities by prospective adopters during placement.

HELPFUL BOOKS

Effective Adoption Panels (6th edn.) by Jenifer Lord and Deborah Cullen, BAAF, 2013
Primarily aimed at adoption workers and panel members. Full of information about the roles and responsibilities of panel members.

Effective Adoption and Fostering Panels in Scotland by Marjorie Morrison, BAAF, 2013
A guide for social workers and panel members on the operation of panels in Scotland.

Prospective Adopters Attending Adoption Panel by Jenifer Lord, BAAF, 2011 (2nd edn.)
Guidance for panel members on the prospective adopters' role at panel, the input they can have, and how to evaluate their contribution.

Who is on the adoption panel?

The panel usually consists of about five to ten people, including:

- the Chair – a person who has experience in adoption work and is independent of the agency

- one social worker with experience of adoption

- sometimes a member of the agency's management committee or local authority's social services committee

- usually the medical adviser

- some "independent" persons who are not members or employees of the agency or local authority. Where possible these people should include people with personal experience of adoption.

A panel is only quorate when at least five of its members are present, and this must include the Chair or Vice-chair, a social worker and at least one independent member if the Vice-chair is chairing and not independent. Adoption Agencies Regulations require that applicants be invited to attend the panel meeting.

The composition, terms of reference and functions of an adoption panel are set out in the Adoption Agencies Regulations 2005, the Adoption Agencies and Independent Review of Determinations (Amendment) Regulations 2011, the Adoption Agencies (Panel and Consequential Amendments) Regulations 2012, the Adoption Agencies (Miscellaneous Amendments) Regulations 2013, and statutory Adoption Guidance 2011, revised in 2013.

What issues will the panel consider when considering the application?

The panel will consider the Prospective Adopter's Report provided by your social worker, as well as information about your statutory eligibility and suitability (including marital status, nationality, domicile, criminal records, and financial considerations). Within this context, panel members will focus on the following specific issues.

- **Your reasons for adopting** – panel members will want to be sure that you understand and can address any relevant emotional issues that have led you to adoption.

  For example, why have you applied to adopt? Do you understand your motivation to care for a child? Are you able to identify your own needs and expectations regarding adoption? Have you dealt with issues of infertility (if applicable)?

  This is not to say that you must have resolved all such issues, but that you are able to identify and understand them, and to deal with resulting feelings.

- **The child and birth family** – do you understand the intense emotional needs of children (of any age) who have experienced trauma, separation or loss? What are your feelings regarding the birth parents and their inability to care for the child? Will you be ready to deal with needs that are not yet identified in the child?

- **Your family structure** – do you have a support network you can rely on? Are there other children in the family? The child's position in the family can affect his or her ability to adjust to the family and can be affected by the child's particular emotional needs. Also, research has shown that there is a greater risk that the placement will not thrive if the child is placed in a family that has other children close to him or her in age.

- **Your relationships** – if you are divorced or have had previous partnerships, panel members will consider whether or not there is a pattern of relationship difficulties that could be repeated in the future and, if so, what plans you would then make for the child.

- **Your age** – while law prohibits discrimination on the basis of age, the panel will want to "maximise" the chances that you will remain fit and healthy well into the child's young adulthood. In order to adopt, you must be at least 21 years old.

- **Your current health** – lifestyle and medical issues will be considered for their impact on you and your family. If you have particular concerns, it is best to talk to your social worker about them.

- **If you have a criminal record** – See *Who Can Adopt?*, p16.

The panel will also consider issues of culture, "race" and ethnicity; contact with the birth family; financial requirements (e.g. financial support before and after adoption, settling in grants [see Section 2]); and requirements for other adoption support.

The panel makes a recommendation, which you will usually be told about immediately. It may also give advice to the agency about the range of your approval, i.e. age range and number of children. The agency's decision should be made within seven working days of receipt of the panel's recommendation and final set of minutes.

5 You are linked and matched with a child

Once you have been approved as suitable to adopt a child, the agency must prepare a written matching agreement with you, setting out the matching process and your role in identifying a possible child for placement with you. It must also refer you, with your agreement, to the Adoption Register immediately, or within three months, unless a link with a specific child is being considered. Your social worker will begin the process of matching you with a child or children and you can be proactive by looking in *Be My Parent* or *Children Who Wait*. In some cases, a child may have been identified before you began the adoption process (for example, foster carers adopting a foster child; grandparents or other birth relatives adopting a child; or applicants who apply to adopt a specific child).

An adoption agency can only match you with a child who has been "authorised" by the granting of a placement order or the giving of formal consent to placement for adoption by the child's parents (called a section 19 consent).

Your social worker will visit you to discuss the details of a prospective child. If you express an interest in pursuing adoption of the child, the child's social worker and possibly the foster carer/s will also arrange to visit you. You must be given the Child's Permanence Report (CPR).

During these visits, it is important to discuss openly all relevant details about the child. Do not hesitate to ask questions because you fear it might seem "impolite" or "intrusive". After all, you are making a decision that will affect the child and you for the rest of your lives. If you decide not to proceed with a match for a child, you must return the Child's Permanence Report to the agency.

....

TERMS YOU NEED TO KNOW

The Child's Permanence Report (CPR) gives detailed information about the child, such as a physical description, his or her background, personality traits and currently known needs – educational, emotional, physical, health and development, etc. The social worker can provide valuable information and insight into the child's history, current relationships and behaviours.

Your questions answered...

What happens if we're not recommended for approval by the panel?
It is not the panel that will make the final decision but the agency; the agency is not required to follow the panel's recommendation (see flowchart on p18).

What happens if we're not approved by the local authority or the agency? If the agency or local authority proposes not to approve your application, it must notify you in writing and must give its reasons. You must also be told if the panel's recommendation was different from the agency's proposal. You then have 40 days in England and Wales to make representations to the agency OR request a review of the agency's proposal by the IRM but *not to both* (see below for details of the IRM). If you do not present your views, the agency can make its decision. If you make representations to the agency decision maker within 40 days in England and Wales, he or she may refer you back to the panel.

If the case is presented again to the panel, the panel must give the case fresh consideration. Alternatively, the agency may choose (but is not obligated) to present the case to a different adoption panel (some agencies have more than one panel, or may present cases to panels of other agencies). The agency's decision after this second consideration will then be final.

A final decision can also be made, after considering your views, without the case going back to panel. You may also raise general concerns about the process with First4Adoption.

If you are still unhappy about the process, you may use the agency's representation and complaints procedure.

How long does our "approval" last? Adoption Agencies Regulations require that the approval should be reviewed at least annually until a child is placed (at least every two years in Wales) or whenever the agency considers a review to be necessary. Your agency should give you clear information about this.

It is important that agency staff have regular contact with approved adopters who are waiting to be matched with a child. Panels have a useful role in reviewing the circumstances of waiting adopters and should receive regular, brief updating reports, perhaps every three or six months.

Summary of your rights throughout the approval process

- You must be shown a copy of the social worker's assessment section of the Prospective Adopter's Report (not including the medical information and references).

- You must be given an opportunity of at least five working days to comment on the assessment before it is presented to panel.

- You must be invited to attend the panel meeting.

- If the agency proposes not to approve your application, it must notify you in writing, and give its reasons.

- You must also be told if the panel's recommendation is different from the local authority's or agency's proposal.

- You have 40 days to present your views to the local authority or agency OR to apply to the IRM.

- If you contact the local authority or agency, it then decides whether or not to re-present the case to the panel. It may elect to present the information to a different panel.

- If the same panel considers the case, it must give it *fresh* consideration.

- If you request a review by the IRM, your case will be considered by an IRM panel, which will make a recommendation.

- The local authority or agency's decision after this second consideration will be final.

Social workers are required to provide the most up-to-date and complete information available.

Independent Review Mechanism (IRM)
Unit 4, Pavilion Business Park
Royds Hall Road
Wortley
Leeds LS12 6AJ
Tel: 0845 450 3956
Email: irm@baaf.org.uk
www.independentreviewmechanism.org.uk

This is an independent review process, conducted by a panel. It is operated by BAAF under contract to the DfE. It applies to cases where an adoption agency in England is proposing not to approve, or to terminate the approval of, adoptive parents. If you receive notification in writing from your adoption agency that it proposes not to approve you, or to terminate your approval as an adoptive parent (this is called a "qualifying determination"), you can apply for a review EITHER to the agency (see above) OR to the IRM, but not to both.

If you decided to apply to the IRM, you must contact the IRM within 40 days of the written notification from the agency. The IRM will arrange for your case to be heard by an independent IRM panel, which you can attend.

The panel will make a recommendation which will go to your agency. The agency will then make the final decision.

Independent Review Mechanism Cymru
7 Cleeve House
Lambourne Crescent
Cardiff CF14 5GP
Tel: 0845 873 1305
Email: irm@irmcymru.org.uk
www.irmcymru.org.uk

This is run by BAAF under contract to the Welsh Assembly Government and is available to people assessed by adoption agencies in Wales. It operates in a very similar way to the IRM in England.

The child's social worker should also discuss contact and support arrangements, the child's need for services after placement and adoption, for example, extra support in school, therapy, etc. There should also be discussion with you about the support that you are likely to need and about the services which the agency will provide, and proposed arrangements for contact (if any).

Adoption Support Services Regulations 2005 and accompanying Guidance place a duty on local authorities to assess the likely adoption support needs of a child when adoption becomes the plan and to make and agree an adoption support plan with prospective adopters when a potential match is being considered.

A proposed adoption support plan should be discussed with you before the match goes to panel and the proposals for adoption support should be included in the Adoption Placement Report. Once the match has been approved, you and the child's agency should finalise the arrangements for the support that the child and you are likely to need after placement and adoption. This could include, for example, financial support, the provision of therapy for the child, support groups or workshops for you, training for you to meet the child's needs, or respite care.

The medical adviser should provide a written health report on each child being considered for adoption. This report should include comments on birth history, family history, past medical history, current physical and mental health and behaviour and, if age appropriate, a developmental assessment. This report should assess the future implications for the child

HELPFUL PUBLICATIONS/WEBSITES

Resources listing children who are waiting to be adopted

The following publications and websites profile children who need families. If these publications feature a child you are interested in parenting, the child's social worker will still have to make sure that you are the right family for that child.

Be My Parent/www.bemyparent.org.uk

A monthly newspaper and online service produced by BAAF (see Appendix 2) which features photographs and a brief description of children of all ages and backgrounds from all over the UK. The online edition also contains videoclips and enhanced profiles. Available by subscription.

Children Who Wait/www.adoptionuk.org

A listing of children needing new families throughout the UK, updated monthly and also available online. Available by becoming a member of Adoption UK. See Appendix 2 for details on contacting Adoption UK.

Adoption agencies also use **local or specialist media** to feature children needing adoption, e.g. *The Voice*, a weekly aimed at black communities, frequently features black children to attract the interest of black families. Occasionally, for example, during **National Adoption Week** in November, television and national newspapers also alert the public to the needs of children needing adoption and may feature certain children.

of their health history, and previous family and social situation, including their experiences in the care system.

It is good practice for the medical adviser to meet with prospective adopters to share all appropriate health information and to discuss the needs of the child with whom you are matched. It is also good practice to provide a written report of this meeting.

THE ADOPTION REGISTER FOR ENGLAND AND WALES

The Adoption Register has two major elements:

- A computer database that stores details of children awaiting adoption where their own agency has not been able to find the right adoptive family, and details of approved adopters awaiting a placement where their own agency has not been able to match them with appropriate children; and

- A staff team of experienced database operators and family placement social workers who will look at the information to see whether they can suggest possible "matches" between children and prospective adopters.

Agencies refer to the Register those children who have been authorised to be placed for adoption but where there is not already a link identified locally which is being actively pursued. The children will be referred at the latest by three months after the agency has formally decided that a child should be placed for adoption and either:

- a placement order has been granted; or

- an application has been made for a placement order and all required consents, including that of the court, have been obtained; or

- the consent to placement for adoption has been obtained from parents with parental responsibility.

If you are a prospective adopter, you will be able to contact the Register direct on the helpline (see below). Once your identity has been checked, the Register will confirm that your details have been referred to them, give you information about the number of times your details have been sent out to social workers for consideration, and give you general advice. If your details have been sent out for consideration but a link is not being pursued, you can contact your social worker and ask about the reasons given by the child's social worker for not pursuing the link.

Agencies can refer prospective adopters to the Adoption Register as soon as they have been approved by the agency and will usually do this if it seems unlikely that the adopters will be matched quickly with a suitable child in their own region. Agencies must refer prospective adopters (with their consent) to the Adoption Register three months after they have been approved if there is not a match with an identified child being actively pursued. You can decide that you do not wish to give your consent to referral to the Adoption Register but this will, of course, reduce the opportunity for you to be matched with an appropriate child.

If your agency has not already sent your details to the Adoption Register, you will be able to contact the Register and complete a referral form. You must wait to do this until at least three months after the date on which your agency approved you as an adopter. The Register staff will then contact your agency and arrange your referral.

Matching children with adoptive families

Once your details have been recorded on the Register database, a search will be undertaken to identify child(ren) who match your approval profile. Relevant details of your family, including a written description (profile) and details of your approving agency will be sent to the child(ren)'s social worker who will consider the proposed link further. Information about your family can initially be sent out up to five times to different social workers

One of the keys to successful introductions is... the capacity of the adults concerned to work together in the interests of the child...This means acknowledging that adopters bring skills and knowledge to the placement process. Their experience of the child may be different from that of previous carers, as permanence brings with it a far more loaded emotional agenda. Listening to, reviewing with and empowering prospective adoptive parents will generally facilitate positive outcomes.

S. Byrne, *Linking and Introductions*, BAAF, 2000, p.10

What happens during the introductions?

During the introductions, you will normally first meet the child at his or her foster home. You will spend a few hours with the child, initially, and gradually spend more time on successive days. You can take this time to observe the child's interactions with the foster carer and to discuss the child's general behaviour and habits (eating, dressing, playing, likes/dislikes, etc).

After visiting the child in the foster home, the child will spend time at your house during the day and, eventually, may stay overnight and return to the foster home the next day. The length of time the introductory period takes depends entirely upon you and the child – older children may take longer to adjust to you (and you to them). You may also feel pressured by school term dates, holidays or other activities. But "speeding up" the process to meet these dates may not be in your or the child's best interests.

You can help the child adjust to the idea of moving in with you. Once you have been matched with the child, you will be asked to create a book for the child that tells about yourself and your family, and what it is like to live at your house. You can include photos of yourself, your home, family, neighbours, pets, and daily or favourite activities. It is helpful, especially for young children, to enable the child to "interact" with the book (by providing crayons or stickers with the book), thus making it his or her own (see *Helpful books* below).

Oh, the stress of it!

Spending time with the child at the foster carer's home can be a stressful experience for prospective adopters. You undoubtedly will be anxious to establish your own relationship with the child and you may find it difficult if the child is fairly attached to the foster carer. In addition, you may not agree with various ways in which the foster carer interacts with the child. It is important to remember, however, that these first visits are meant for you to observe the child so you can determine how best to meet his or her needs. Candid discussions with the foster carer(s) can give you valuable insight into the child that will help everyone in the long run.

8 The child moves in (i.e. is placed with you)

In preparation for the child moving to your home, you will have a **final planning meeting** with your social worker, the child's social worker, foster carer/s, teachers – and anyone else significantly involved with the child – to discuss the placement date and to confirm details of the Adoption Placement Plan.

The Adoption Placement Plan

When an agency has decided on a placement it must provide 'as soon as possible' a *written adoption placement plan* to the prospective adopters.

Content of Adoption Placement Plan – Schedule 5, Adoption Agency Regulations 2005

1 Whether the child is to be placed under a **placement order** or **consent of the parent/guardian**.

2 The arrangements for **preparing the child** and the prospective adopters for the placement.

3 The **date on which it is proposed to place the child** with the prospective adopters.

4 The arrangements for **review** of the placement.

5 **Whether the parental responsibility for the prospective adopters is to be restricted** and if so, the extent to which it is to be restricted.

6 **The support services** to be provided for the adoptive family.

7 **The agency's arrangements for allowing any person contact** with the child, the form of contact, the arrangements for supporting contact and the name and details of the person responsible for facilitating the contact arrangements (if applicable).

8 **The dates on which the child's life story book and later-life letter are to be provided** by the adoption agency to the prospective adopters.

9 Details of **any other arrangements** that need to be made.

10 **Contact details** for the child's social worker, the prospective adopters' social worker and out-of-hours contacts.

This final planning meeting will help everyone involved to understand each others' roles, responsibilities and expectations during the post-placement period. For example, you will want to know:

- the extent to which both social workers will be involved with the child during the placement;

- what contact (if any) the child will have with the birth family;

- if the child will have any continued contact with foster carers;

- what arrangements need to be made with other services (health, education) and who should arrange them; and

- what adoption support services are to be provided and when and how they are to be provided.

Settling-in grants

These are available for most children if they are needed. For details about these grants and about other financial support, see Section 2.

important to remember that, as children grow up, they may seek to have contact with birth parents and relatives, and may search for them. See Section 4 for more information about resources for adopted people who are seeking contact with birth relatives.

When is the best time for the child to move?

There really is no "best" or "worst" time for placement. Generally, you will want to arrange moving in to suit the child. For school-age children, this means thinking about whether the child will need to change schools and when will be the best time to do this. Moving in during school holidays may not be ideal, because there will be less structure and routine in the child's life, which he or she may find unsettling. You and the child will also have constant interaction during holiday periods, which may prove difficult for both of you at the start of a placement.

The child generally benefits if your life continues "as normal" after moving in. "Celebrating" the event with large parties or exotic holidays will disrupt the child's normal routine and will make it harder for the child to adjust to the new family and surroundings. After all, returning from holiday or settling down after a party will entail another "change" for a child who has just experienced one of the most stressful changes in his or her young life.

You will need to arrange:

- an appointment with your GP and/or practice nurse to introduce the child and to discuss any questions you might have about the child's health records;

- visits with schools or playgroups (if the child will have to change to a new one).

Your local authority must inform your GP and the education department of the child's placement with you. If the child is three years old or younger, your local health visitor should arrange to visit you. If this does not happen, contact your GP's surgery to make the appointment.

You may also wish to consult the GP with whom your child was registered while he or she was in foster care.

You should receive your child's health record book from your social worker. This lists your child's NHS number, immunisations, a growth record and other significant health information. If this record book is not available, ask your GP to provide a new one for your child. You will also have health information about the child in the Child's Permanence Report.

Having a child move in will almost be like giving birth. Do I have any legal basis for taking time off work?

Yes. Statutory adoption leave and statutory adoption pay (SAP) and also statutory paternity leave and statutory paternity pay (SPP) are now available.

SAP and adoption leave are available to employees (male or female) adopting a child. They could be adopting on their own, or with their spouse or civil partner.

- SAP is paid for a maximum of 39 weeks at the lower rate of £136.78 (currently) or 90% of average weekly earnings.

- Adoption leave is available for 52 weeks but only the first 39 weeks are covered by SAP.

- To qualify for adoption leave the adopter must have completed 26 weeks continuous service with their employer by the end of the week in which they are notified of being matched with a child.

An adopter who wishes to receive SAP and take adoption leave will need to give their employer documentary evidence to confirm that they are adopting a child through an adoption agency. You will need a Matching Certificate, issued by your adoption agency, once you have been formally matched with a child.

Statutory paternity pay (SPP) and paternity leave are available to employees (male or female) who are the partner of someone adopting a child on their own or adopting a child with their spouse or civil partner.

- SPP and paternity leave can be taken for one or two whole weeks.

- SPP is paid at the lower rate of £136.78 (currently) or 90% of average weekly earnings.

- To qualify for paternity leave the employee must have completed 26 weeks continuous service with their employer by the end of the week in which the adopter is notified of having been matched with a child.

An adopter (or their partner) who wishes to take SPP and paternity leave will need to give their employer evidence of their entitlement and will need information from the adoption agency for this. This is the Matching Certificate, described above.

If a couple is adopting a child jointly, the couple must choose who takes the SAP and adoption leave and who takes the SPP and paternity leave. If the person who was on adoption leave decides to go back to work early and forfeit the remaining leave and pay, the partner claiming paternity leave may be eligible for up to 26 weeks paid Additional Paternity leave.

SAP and adoption leave and SPP and paternity leave are not normally available to foster carers adopting without the approval of the child's local authority or to step-parents who adopt a child – this is because these are not *agency* adoptions.

Employees who adopt a child from overseas (or whose partner does) may be eligible for SAP and adoption leave and SPP and paternity leave – the entitlements are the same as for those adopting a child in the UK.

HELPFUL BOOKS

Adopted Children Speaking by Caroline Thomas and Verna Beckford, BAAF, 1999
This book offers moving and poignant testimonies and valuable insights into what children feel about adoption, including waiting for a family, moving in, and the involvement of the courts.

Adopters on Adoption: Reflections on parenthood and children by David Howe, BAAF, 1996
An absorbing collection of personal stories that covers assessment and preparation, feelings towards birth family members, parenting issues and the experience of adopting.

The Colours in Me: Writing and poetry by adopted children and young people edited by Perlita Harris, BAAF, 2008
A unique collection of poetry, prose and artwork by over 80 young contributors – ranging from 4–20 years of age – who reveal what it feels like and what it means to be adopted. Also available, a DVD containing readings from *The Colours in Me*.

Could You be my Parent? Adoption and fostering stories edited by Leonie Sturge-Moore, BAAF, 2005
A collection of articles and interviews taken from BAAF's family-finding newspaper, *Be My Parent*, which create a fascinating snapshot of the process of adoption and foster care.

The Dynamics of Adoption: Social and personal perspectives edited by Amal Treacher and Ilan Katz, Jessica Kingsley Publishers, 2000
A collection of essays about numerous aspects of adoption. This book is not a practical guide to adoption, rather a collection of thoughts about aspects of adoption.

Intercountry Adoption: Developments, trends and perspectives edited by Peter Selman, BAAF, 2000
An anthology that explores several aspects of intercountry adoption from a variety of perspectives including those of "sending" countries, "receiving" countries, adopters, adopted people and researchers.

Can we travel outside of the UK for a holiday with our child, if he or she has been placed with us, but the adoption has not yet been legalised in the courts?

Yes. If the adoption order has not yet been made, you must inform children's services of your intention to travel abroad. They will provide a letter giving you permission to take the child abroad. You must carry this letter with you, to avoid any difficulties with immigration officers who may question why you have a different surname from that of your child.

If your child does not have a passport, you must have one issued in his or her birth name. You cannot take the child out of the UK for more than one month without the permission of the court or the permission of the birth parents with parental responsibilities.

10 Settling in and post-placement adoption support

'... there is no single factor that leads to success or to instability in a placement, but the way in which several factors combine and interact.'

R. Parker, *Adoption Now: Messages from Research*, Department of Health, 1999, p.15

As your child settles in to live with you and your family, you will continue to receive support from your social worker and from the child's social worker.

Statutory visits

The child's social worker (and possibly your social worker) will visit the child at your home within the first week. After that, they must visit at least once a week until the first review at four weeks to see how the child and you are settling in together. The social worker will arrange a statutory review within four weeks of the placement. Another review will follow three months after the first, and then six-monthly until the adoption order is granted. It is important to view these visits as a useful means of gathering support and information, rather than an intrusive invasion of your privacy. You and the child will gain the most benefit from these visits if you are candid with the social worker and raise the questions or issues that concern you.

What should I do if the child behaves badly during the social worker's visit?

Don't be afraid to treat your child "normally" – as you would if the social worker was not present. Most social workers have had many years' experience with children and will be well aware that the child may be very attention seeking or may behave badly during these visits. It will help your child if your response to him or her is consistent, no matter what the circumstances.

What do older children feel when being placed with a new family?

It is always helpful to try to put yourself in the child's shoes. How would you have felt, for example, at the age of four, upon moving in with a family of people you had met only a few weeks ago? The child may feel anxious, worried, perhaps somewhat frightened. He or she will need to understand the moving-in process in his or her "own" way. Social workers can help you and the child by giving the child as much information as possible in an "age-appropriate" way, explaining the purpose of the "introductions", and by providing information about you. Many foster carers also prepare the child for this event from the moment he or she arrives in their home.

You can also talk with your social worker about how best to minimise the child's anxiety, for example, by continuing contact with the foster family, the child's friends and activities, etc.

Legal and financial matters

2

In this section:

→ Gain a general understanding of the current laws and regulations concerning adoption and how they may affect you

→ Learn about your legal rights throughout the adoption process and afterwards, and about the rights of the child and the birth parents

→ Find out about the various costs involved with adoption and the financial assistance that may be available to some applicants

TERMS YOU MAY NEED TO KNOW

Accommodation/accommodated – England and Wales Under Section 20 of the Children Act 1989, the local authority is required to 'provide accommodation' for children in need in certain circumstances. The local authority does not acquire parental responsibility merely by accommodating a child and the arrangements for the child must normally be agreed with the parent(s), who, subject to certain circumstances, are entitled to remove the child from local authority accommodation at any time. They retain parental responsibility. A child who is accommodated is a looked after child.

Accommodation/accommodated – Scotland Under Section 25 of the Children (Scotland) Act 1995, the local authority must 'provide accommodation' for children in certain circumstances and may also do so in other situations. Normally, the accommodation is provided by agreement with the parent(s); they can then remove the child at any time in most circumstances. Parental responsibilities remain with the parent(s). A child accommodated under section 25 is a looked after child.

Adoption Order A court order that transfers sole parental responsibility to the adoptive parent/s. An adoption order usually cannot be made unless the child and adopters attend the adoption order hearing at court (unless there are special circumstances preventing the child or one of the adopters from attending). The court can make an order for contact along with the adoption order, although this is very rare.

If the court refuses the adoption order, the court may make another order under the Adoption and Children Act 2002 or the Children Act 1989 – including, for example, a special guardianship order, a residence order, or revising of a placement order.

Brief Report – England A short report taken to an adoption panel when the agency decides early on that it has serious concerns about an adopter's application, but the applicant disagrees and wishes to proceed. The panel can either recommend that the application proceeds to full assessment, or that it is turned down. The recommendation is then accepted or not by the agency decision-maker. If he or she makes a qualifying determination that the applicant should be turned down, the applicant may apply to the Independent Review Mechanism (IRM).

Care Order A court order giving a local authority parental responsibility for a child which is shared with the child's birth parents, but enables the local authority to make the major decisions about a child's life, such as with whom and where the child should live, and consent to routine medical treatment.

Concurrent planning This is the term given to a very small number of schemes currently operating. Children, usually babies or toddlers, for whom there is a chance that they might return home to their birth family, are placed with families who will foster them with this aim. However, the foster carers are also approved as adopters and will adopt the child, should the planned return home not be successful. In this way, the moves that a child may otherwise have to make are minimised. These schemes have to be run with the agreement and co-operation of the local court and to tight timescales.

Contact Order When a child is a subject of a placement order or section 19 consent to placement for adoption, there is no duty to provide contact but a contact order can be made under section 26 of the Adoption and Children Act 2002.

A section 8 contact order can be applied for or granted with an adoption order or after an adoption order is granted.

Emergency Protection Order A court order allowing the local authority, in an emergency, either to keep a child in a safe place (such as a hospital or foster home) or to remove a child (e.g. from a home) if it is considered the child is suffering, or is at risk of suffering, significant harm. The local authority must then apply to the court for a care order within the next seven days, if it is believed the child should remain in care to safeguard his or her welfare.

For both an emergency protection order and a care order to be granted by a court, the local authority must satisfy the court that the child is suffering, or is at risk of suffering, significant harm, attributable to an unsatisfactory standard of parental care.

Children's Guardian An officer from CAFCASS (Children and Family Court Advisory and Support Service) appointed by a court when:

i   an application is made by a local authority for a care order or a supervision order for a child; or

ii when an application is made for a placement order or an adoption order that is opposed by birth parents.

A Children's Guardian may also be appointed in adoption proceedings in other circumstances, such as where there is a dispute about contact arrangements after adoption or the child does not wish to be adopted or is being adopted by relatives. The Children's Guardian is an experienced qualified social worker independent of the local authority.

The Children's Guardian conducts an independent investigation to establish whether or not the care order or placement order applied for is in the interests of the child. He or she meets with the child, the social worker/s and the birth parents. He or she is only likely to meet adopters if parents have been given leave to oppose the making of the adoption order, there is a dispute about contact after the adoption, or the child is being adopted by relatives. The Children's Guardian may also make other relevant investigations, if necessary. He or she then presents the findings to the court, which will then either grant or refuse the order applied for.

HELPFUL ORGANISATIONS

Children and Family Courts Advisory and Support Service (CAFCASS)

Practitioners who provide advice to courts about the welfare of children. CAFCASS administers the children's guardians service.

6th floor, Sanctuary Buildings
Great Smith Street
London SW1P 3BT
Tel: 0844 353 4332
Email: webenquiries@cafcass.gov.uk
www.cafcass.gov.uk

Child Law Advice Line

0808 802 0008

Community Legal Service

A government initiative designed to ensure that everyone has access to quality legal advice and information, including by funding legal costs for those on a very low income without significant capital. The service can be provided by Citizens Advice Bureaux (CABs), solicitors' firms and legal advice centres that have been awarded the Community Legal Service Quality mark.

You can find the *Community Legal Service Directory* at your local library. It lists all the law firms and advice centres which have the Quality Mark, and indicates whether firms offer free advice or if they charge.

Tel: 0845 345 4345 for advice and information about CLS providers or about the CLS directory.
www.legalservices.gov.uk

Coram Children's Legal Centre

Specialises in law and policy affecting children and young people. Produces information sheets and booklets. In addition to policy and campaign work, CLC also provides an advice and information service (free and confidential legal advice).

Helpline: 0808 802 0008 (free legal advice)
www.childrenslegalcentre.com

Family Rights Group

A national organisation that advises families who are in contact with children's services, about the care of their children.

The Print House
18 Ashwin Street
London E8 3DL
Tel: 020 7923 2628
Advice line: 0808 801 0366
Email: advice@frg.org.uk
www.frg.org.uk

www.family-solicitors.co.uk

An online information service that provides advice and specific information about adoption, and lists solicitors who specialise in adoption and other aspects of family law.

www.compactlaw.co.uk

An online legal and information service that provides specific information about adoption law.

- other financial support that might include respite care, emergency support, domestic help, therapy for the child, or other costs involved during the placement.

If the child is less than five years old, placed singly and without significant special needs or disabilities, it is unlikely that most of these expenses will be met by local authorities or that ongoing financial support will be paid.

State benefits for a child's special needs (such a Disability Living Allowance or Carer's Allowance) may be available to adopters from placement. Child benefit is payable from the date of placement for adoption, and tax credits can be claimed.

TERMS YOU MAY NEED TO KNOW

Fostering allowance – financial support payable by local authorities to foster carers (not to prospective adopters). There are nationally recommended rates for foster carers but these do vary considerably between local authorities.

Settling-in financial support – most local authorities will make available a settling-in grant. This is a discretionary grant and you can ask your social worker how to apply for it.

Is regular financial support available after an adoption order?

Adoption allowance

Regular financial support can be paid on a weekly or monthly basis to adoptive parents before and after the adoption order is granted. This allowance is permitted under the Adoption Support Services (Local Authorities) Regulations 2005 (and equivalent regulations in Wales). Financial support is designed to facilitate adoptions of children who might otherwise not be adopted, due to the financial cost to the adopters. The allowance is not taken into account for income-related benefits and income tax.

According to the Adoption Support Services Regulations 2005, financial support may be paid if one or more of the following circumstances exist:

- the child has not been placed with the adoptive parents for adoption, and financial support is necessary to ensure that the adoptive parents can look after the child if placed with them;

- the child has been placed with the adoptive parents for adoption, and financial support is necessary to ensure that the adoptive parents can continue to look after the child;

- the child has been adopted, and financial support is necessary to ensure that the adoptive parents can continue to look after the child;

- the local authority is satisfied that the child has established a strong and important relationship with the adoptive parent before the adoption order is made;

- it is desirable that the child be placed with the same adoptive parents as his or her brother or sister (whether of the full blood or half blood) or with a child with whom he or she has previously shared a home;

- the child needs special care which requires a greater expenditure of resources by reason of illness, disability, emotional or behavioural difficulties or the continuing consequences of past abuse or neglect;

- on account of the age, sex or ethnic origin of the child it is necessary for the local authority to make special arrangements to facilitate the placement of the child for adoption.

The amount payable as regular financial support is determined by the local authority, which takes into account the adopters' financial resources and commitments (not including the value of their home).

Financial support paid after adoption must not include any element of fee or reward which the carers were receiving as foster carers of the child. However, the exception to this is when foster carers wish to adopt a child whom they are fostering. They may continue to receive financial support, which includes a reward element for two years and, in some situations, for longer, after an adoption order.

Adopters receiving regular financial support must inform the local authority of changes in their financial or other circumstances and supply an annual statement of their finances. Financial support must be reviewed annually.

Payment of financial support will not affect other benefits you receive, such as Income Support, except the element for the child. Contact the Benefit Enquiry Line (0800 882 200) for more information.

What about a lump-sum payment?

Instead of regular ongoing financial support, the local authority may agree with you to pay you a single lump-sum payment or a series of lump-sum payments, to meet specific assessed needs.

Can I apply for financial support after an adoption order?

Yes. The Adoption Support Services Regulations 2005 provide that adoptive families can ask for their need for adoption support, including financial support, to be assessed at any point before or after the adoption order until their child is 18 and ceases full-time education or training. Local authorities have a duty to do an assessment if asked. You would need to apply to the local authority which placed the child with you unless it is more than three years since the adoption order. If this is the case, you need to apply to the local authority where you live. However, if you were receiving regular financial support before the adoption order and continue to receive it, the responsibility for that financial support continues with the placing agency, wherever you live.

Your entitlements regarding financial support

There is currently a lack of consistency among local authorities in assessment and payment of financial support.

However, local authorities are *required* to:

- consider if financial support should be paid;
- inform adopters about available financial support;
- give adopters written notice of the proposed decision about financial support;
- hear representation from adopters about financial support;
- review the financial support annually.

If you believe your needs have not been fairly assessed or if you have other complaints about the adoption support, use your local authority complaints procedure in the first instance. If you still are not satisfied, you may contact your Local Authority Ombudsman.

The placing local authority has responsibility for adoption support for three years from the making of the adoption order. After this, responsibility moves to the local authority where the adoptive family lives. However, as Adoption Guidance 9.20 states:

'The placing local authority is responsible for the continued payment of financial support agreed before the adoption order is made. It is important that this provision is not misinterpreted as justification for a decision to pay ongoing financial support for a period limited to three years from the making of the adoption order. Any decision on the provision of support must be based on the needs and resources of the child and family. This applies equally to a decision about the period for which financial support is payable.'

Other benefits

The local authority cannot duplicate the financial help you might receive from state benefits (and tax credits). Other types of benefits may be payable to adoptive parents by the Benefits Agency, as for any child in their family, under certain circumstances. These benefits are not automatically payable if you have an adopted child with physical, mental or emotional difficulties. However, it is worth knowing which benefits exist and are available in case you require financial support at some point in the life of your adopted child. You will need to find out which are means tested. These benefits currently include:

- **Disability Living Allowance (DLA)** Some families now receive DLA for children who have attachment difficulties. This is the exception, not the rule, however, and you will have to apply to your local benefits office in order to receive this payment.

- **Carer's Allowance** Adoptive parents, like all parents of children with disabilities, may be eligible for Carer's Allowance *in addition* to Disability Living Allowance, as long as one parent is not in full-time employment or earning more than £50 per week (irrespective of the partner's income). Many adoptive parents (usually mothers) are unable to take jobs because the needs of their children are so immense and because childcare arrangements are generally unable to meet the children's specific needs.

HELPFUL RESOURCES

For information about benefits, contact:

- the Benefit Enquiry Line 0800 882 200;

- your local post office (applications and information about various available benefits);

- your local Citizens Advice Bureau (offers advice and information) – check your local phone book for the Bureau nearest you;

- your local authority's welfare rights department (usually located within social services);

- *Community Care* magazine – www.communitycare.co.uk – has articles on the benefits system.

Am I entitled to leave during the adoption of my child?

Yes – both statutory and adoption leave and pay and also statutory paternity leave and pay are now available (see Section 1).

Benefits provisions of the Carers and Disabled Children Act 2000

If your child has a physical or mental disability as defined by this Act, then you or your child may be eligible for:

- direct payments to 16- and 17-year-old young people who have a disability;

- direct payments to carers to meet their own assessed needs – this may mean that parents of a disabled child could receive a direct payment, rather than use the services provided by the local council, perhaps because they think existing services are not suitable or appropriate for their child.

Contact your local Benefits Agency for more information about these benefits and see Section 4.

Schooling and education

3

The Mental Health Needs of Looked After Children edited by Joanna Richardson and Carol Joughin, Gaskell, 2000.
Presents information on a range of mental health issues affecting children in care. Incorporates opinions and perspectives of children in the care system, and includes professional information and guidance regarding the young people's views.

Promoting Children's Mental Health within Early Years and School Settings
A booklet produced by the Department for Education (DfE) to help teachers and other people working co-operatively with health professionals, to promote children's mental health. It provides examples of mental health initiatives taking place within schools and gives advice on how to help children who are having difficulties or who have defined mental health problems.

DfE Publications
Tel: 0845 602 2260
www.education.gov.uk/publications-dfe

Special Education Handbook: The law on children with special needs
Explains the process of obtaining a statement of special educational needs and various aspects of the statementing process.
Available from the Advisory Centre for Education.

Special Educational Needs: A guide for parents
Available free from the Department for Education (DfE) publications section.

Special Educational Needs Update
A newsletter published by the DfE and sent to all schools, local education authorities, health authorities, children's services departments, and NHS Trusts in England. For more information contact the DfE.

Tel: 0845 602 2260
www.education.gov.uk/
childrenandyoungpeople/send

Special Needs: A guide for parents and carers of Jewish children with special educational needs
Available from the Board of Deputies of British Jews.

Tel: 020 7543 5400

Websites

Center for Positive Behavioral Intervention and Support
www.pbis.org
Created by the US Department for Education to help schools implement and sustain positive behaviour-intervention programmes.

Department for Education (DfE)
Provides links to various government initiatives for raising standards in education, and provides a database of good practice programmes throughout the country.

www.education.gov.uk

Your child: physical and emotional needs

4

In this section

→ learn about the general effects of trauma and neglect on children

→ examine the emotional and physical difficulties adopted children may experience

→ find out how to access the services your child may need and how to ensure your child receives the help to which he or she is entitled

→ gather information about the organisations and resources which can help you and your child with particular difficulties

Depression Alliance

Promotes greater understanding of depression to reduce the stigma associated with it. Produces booklet, *The Young Person's Guide to Stress*.

20 Great Dover Street
London SE1 4LX
Tel: 0845 123 2320
www.depressionalliance.org

Scottish Health on the Web (SHOW)

Provided by the NHS in Scotland, this site provides general health information, contact details of all NHS Trusts, and links to other websites.
www.show.scot.nhs.uk

UK Youth

A leading national youth development charity which develops, promotes and delivers a range of innovative education programmes in partnership with a national network of organisations. They aim to enable young people to raise their aspirations, realise their potential and have their achievements recognised.
7 Heron Quays
Canary Wharf
London E14 4JB
Tel: 01425 672347
Email: info@ukyouth.org
www.ukyouth.org

YoungMinds

The UK's leading charity committed to improving the emotional wellbeing and mental health of children and young people and empowering their parents and carers. YoungMinds parents' helpline:
0808 802 5544
www.youngminds.org.uk

For adoptive parents

In this section

→ identify and focus on your own particular needs as adoptive parents

→ consider some of the most common emotions adoptive parents encounter and why these feelings occur

→ find the resources, organisations and services that can help you help yourself through the various emotions of the adoption experience

Introduction

By its very nature, adoption is a process that has its ups and its downs. The first four sections of this book describe many of the procedural, financial and emotional pitfalls that can potentially turn a happy experience into a stressful and frustrating nightmare.

The experience of having a child, by birth or by adoption, is always a journey into the unknown – none of us knows if our expected child will have any physical or emotional difficulties. Yet, because adoption is a *process* of bringing a child into your home and family, you can be fairly certain you will encounter some degree of difficulty at some point along the way.

Acceptance is the first step to a "smooth" adoption

The first step in making the experience of adoption as smooth as possible is to accept that adopting a child is different from giving birth to a child. You will have to adjust your preconceptions and your expectations about parenthood and having children. We hope the resources and information provided in this guide will help you cope with the procedural and physical difficulties you might encounter. The emotional difficulties involved in adoption are a different battle altogether – these are the experiences that challenge you and change you. These are the experiences we discuss in this section.

Adoptive parents' needs are important too

Adoption focuses on meeting the needs of a child. But this does not mean we should ignore the needs of adoptive parents. After all, if you do not look after your own physical and emotional needs, you won't be able to provide much help to your child.

Yet, every adoption is an individual event and everyone responds differently to it. So while we can't predict every emotional response you'll have throughout your adoption – and thus offer "answers" to every difficulty – we can describe some *general* feelings that most adopters experience and offer some *general* advice. Although it is difficult to "avoid" having certain experiences and feelings throughout adoption, just being *aware* of the feelings you might have can often help you get through particular experiences more easily.

Let's take a minute to discuss some of the "lows" of the adoptive parent's emotional rollercoaster. Why would this be helpful? If you have not yet adopted, or only recently adopted, it can help you prepare to expect some of these "lows" and, hopefully, to be less surprised if you experience these emotions. If you have already adopted, perhaps reading about some of the most common emotions adoptive parents face as a result of common experiences of the adoption process will reassure you that other adopters have similar feelings. This can help bolster your confidence as an adoptive parent.

Assessing risk and resilience in prospective carers

Research is currently underway to develop effective tools that will enable social workers and others to assess the emotional and psychological resilience of prospective adoptive parents or foster carers. The intent of this research is not to further scrutinise carers, but to ensue that, as adoptive/foster parents, you are matched with a child whose emotional, psychological and/or physical demands will not exceed your abilities to meet such demands. Current studies include:

Attachment style interview (ASI)

This is a standardised assessment tool developed at Royal Holloway, University of London. It can be used to assess the characteristics of carers in terms of their quality of close relationships, social support and security of attachment style. It assesses particularly the adequacy of support and the carer's ability to access support. It should only be used by trained assessors. A number of adoption agencies are now training workers to use the ASI and are finding it useful.

The use of the Adult Attachment Interview: Implications for assessment in adoption and foster care by M. Steele, J. Kaniuk, J. Hodges, C. Haworth and S. Huss.

This research was conducted at the Anna Freud Centre in London. Researchers studied the use of the Adult Attachment Interview (AAI) in assessing attachment in a group of parents who voluntarily adopted children with developmental delays. The AAI is commonly used in researching parent–child relationships, but has not previously been used in the assessment of carers. Contact the centre at www.annafreud.org for more information (see Appendix 2).

Feelings and emotions adoptive parents commonly encounter throughout the adoption experience

"Instant" parenthood

Despite the months (perhaps years) of planning for your adopted child, it is difficult to be fully prepared for the child's arrival in your home. You can easily prepare for your child's physical needs. But being ready for your and your child's emotional responses (no matter what age child you have adopted) is altogether different. This is particularly true for individuals or couples who have not parented a child before – either born to them,

HELPFUL RESOURCES

Parents are Linked (PAL)

This service, co-ordinated by Adoption UK, links people who have particular questions about adoption with people who can provide useful information based upon their own experiences. The service is available to Adoption UK members. As a member, you can phone Adoption UK, register your question(s) with the PAL database, and then be matched with someone who may be able to help you. For more information, contact Adoption UK (see Appendix 2).

fostered or adopted. The first few months after the placement can be a time of joy, but may also bring feelings of guilt, depression, perhaps even panic. The question, 'Have we done the right thing?', might enter your head more than a few times after the child is first placed with you or after the adoption goes through.

It is important, at this stage, to remember you are a new parent or new to parenting this child and have taken on an immense challenge. You may find it helpful to share your true feelings with others – especially with other adoptive parents. It will also be important to give yourself "respite" time away from your child in order to "rest and recoup" from the stresses of parenting an adopted child.

"Sharing" your child

When your child is finally placed with you, it is common to want to immerse the child in your family life – in a sense, to make the child "your own". It can be difficult, at this time, to continually remind yourself that your child is the focus of the adoption process and that you might have to endure some experiences (such as visits with foster carers and/or birth parents) that you may not enjoy, but which may be in the best interests of your child. It can be painful, for example, to see your newly adopted child run to his or her former foster carers' arms for comfort, or to feel your child reject you in favour of other people he or she has known previously. Moreover, children who have attachment difficulties (see Section 4) are experts at manipulating other adults to their own advantage, while rejecting you in the process. When your child is first placed with you, you may feel surprised, confused and frustrated by such experiences.

"Attachment? What attachment?"

There will be times when you may have to face the issue of "love" for your child. Do you "love" him or her? Or do you feel sympathy, empathy, even "caring" and responsibility, rather than unconditional love? You will not be the first adoptive parent to ask yourself these questions. These

HELPFUL BOOKS

Books about attachment difficulties and parenting children who have attachment difficulties (see also Section 4)

Attachment Handbook for Foster Care and Adoption
by Gillian Schofield and Mary Beek, BAAF, 2006

**Attachment Theory, Child Maltreatment and Family Support:
A practice and assessment model** by David Howe *et al*, Macmillan, 1999

Attachment, Trauma and Resilience: Therapeutic caring for children
by Kate Cairns, BAAF, 2002

Building the Bonds of Attachment by Daniel A. Hughes, Jason Aronson Inc, 2006

First Steps in Parenting the Child Who Hurts: Tiddlers & Toddlers
by Caroline Archer, Jessica Kingsley Publishers, 1999

Fostering Attachments: Long-term outcomes in family group care
by Brian Cairns, BAAF, 2004

Next Steps in Parenting the Child Who Hurts: Tykes & Teens
by Caroline Archer, Jessica Kingsley Publishers, 1999

A list of books of interest to families living with, and professionals working with, children with attachment and behavioural difficulties is available from Adoption UK (see Appendix 2).

feelings arise because many children who have been neglected or abused do not exhibit any vulnerability – that is, they do not show any signs that they really "need" parents. So, you may find it hard to love a child who seemingly doesn't "need" you.

In addition, children with attachment difficulties may have behaviours that make you feel rejected. These are times when your commitment as an adoptive parent overrides all other emotions – you stick with it because you believe in what you are doing, you believe in your child, and you believe in your child's capacity to overcome his or her difficulties.

During these times, it is important to seek support from others – social workers, counsellors, mental health professionals, post-adoption support organisations, and other adoptive parents. It is also imperative to acknowledge your own feelings about being an adoptive parent and to remember that, as adoptive parents, we may not have begun our relationship with our children with immediate "love". We may have felt sympathy and care for the child, initially, but in some cases, true love – the ability to love the child when the child pushes rejection right at you – may take years to develop.

HELPFUL RESOURCES

Training and information for parents

Adoption and Attachment – A one-year, part-time training course for social workers, therapists, foster carers and adoptive parents. For more information contact Family Futures (see Appendix 2).

Enhancing Adoptive Parenting: A parenting programme for use with new adopters of challenging children by Alan Rushton and Helen Upright, BAAF, 2012
This parenting manual is written for adoption support workers and intended to make practical and relevant advice available to the many struggling adopters. The programme aims to support the stability of the adoptive placement, to reduce the level of child problems, and enhance parenting skills and understanding, and improve relationships.

Finding a Way Through: Therapeutic caring for children (DVD), Kate Cairns in conversation with John Simmonds. Shows foster carers and adoptive parents ways of reaching out to damaged children. Available for £36 from BAAF (see Appendix 2).

The Impact of Trauma on Children and How Foster Families and Adoptive Families Can Help Them A videotape presentation by Dan Hughes, a psychologist who specialises in helping fostered and adopted children. Dr Hughes discusses how parents can help children develop positive attachments and presents strategies for coping with oppositional behaviour. Available for £80 from Family Futures (see Appendix 2).

It's a Piece of Cake? A parent support programme developed by adopters for adopters Provided by Adoption UK through local authorities. This eight-module course is designed specifically to help adoptive parents gain insight into their children and to help them in their challenging role with their children. Contact Adoption UK for more information (see Appendix 2).

Managing Difficult Behaviour by Clare Pallett *et al* with Eileen Fursland, BAAF, 2008. A unique handbook that provides foster carers and adopters with new skills to help them improve a child's behaviour. Full of useful tips, case examples and exercises.

Remember, also, that many adoptive parents don't have the benefit of a gestation period or a "bonding time" with a young infant. Parents of children adopted after the age of 2½–3 years are presented with a walking, talking individual with his or her own personality, and with the complex effects of early neglect and/or trauma. Consequently, it will take

HELPFUL BOOKS

Related by Adoption: A handbook for grandparents and other relatives (second edition) by Hedi Argent, BAAF, 2011. This is a very useful short book on adoption written for family members on the useful role which they can play.

time for you to develop a deep bond with your child, just as your child will take time to attach to you.

'Let me explain about adoption...'

A while after having a child placed, many parents develop an understanding of their child and learn how to respond to their child's various behaviours. However, problems often arise when trying to help the "outside" world understand their children and their children's needs. Daily life may then become a series of stressful events, when activities, such as dealing with schools, grandparents, even those after-school swimming lessons, become difficult because the people involved don't understand your child's behaviours. You may hesitate to discuss adoption with these people, because you don't want to appear to make "excuses" for your child's behaviour. Often, however, open communication is the best policy. The general public usually is unaware of the effects of early trauma on children. Explaining these effects and "educating" others in how best to respond to your child will not only help your child now, but will also help others respond more positively to your child in the future.

A question of guilt and anger

Parenting a child who has attachment difficulties is tough. At times, your anger and frustration with the child may exceed levels you never thought existed within you. You may then begin to question your abilities as a parent, feel guilty about your own anger and reactions to your child, and may feel inadequate to the task of parenting an adopted child. These feelings can be reinforced when other well-meaning people around us (grandparents, friends, social workers, spouses) do not see or understand the child's behaviours. 'Why are you so "uptight"?', they wonder. 'Why are you so strict with your child?' They don't understand your emotions, because they don't spend the same amount of time with the child as you do and they don't see that your child may have rejecting behaviours that are targeted at you – the main caregiver. These will be times of extreme frustration and anxiety for you. It will be important for you to seek the support of the post-adoption organisations and services available to you.

HELPFUL BOOKS

Talking about Adoption to your Adopted Child (fifth edition) by Marjorie Morrison, BAAF, 2012
A useful guide that explains how and when to explain to your child that he or she is adopted.

Adoption Conversations: What, when and how to tell by Renée Wolfs, BAAF, 2008
Explores the questions adopted children are likely to ask, with suggestions for helpful explanations and age-appropriate answers.

More Adoption Conversations: What, when and how to tell by Renée Wolfs, BAAF, 2010
Explores the problems that adopted teenagers are likely to confront and provides suggestions for helpful solutions and achievable communication methods.

discussion. Just affirming the past in a matter-of-fact way will help your child to incorporate his or her story into their life, and develop a healthy self-image and sense of self.

GOVERNMENT GUIDANCE ABOUT POST-ADOPTION SUPPORT

In 2013, the Government published the Adoption Passport, a short guide which sets out the support services adopters can expect from local authorities. The Passport is available on the First4Adoption website (www.first4adoption.org.uk) and is shown in Appendix 5.

The Adoption Support Services Regulations 2005, the Adoption Guidance 2011, the National Minimum Standards 2011 and the Practice Guidance on Assessing the Support Needs of Adoptive Families all address support issues.

Adoption Guidance states that:

> 'The provision of a range of adoption support services is a crucial element of the statutory framework introduced by the [Adoption and Children] Act [2002]. This is based on the recognition that adoptive children and their families are likely to have a range of additional needs.' Guidance 9.1.

Children and adults affected by adoption receive an assessment of their adoption support needs. Service users confirm that the adoption support service provided met or are meeting their assessed needs. When deciding whether to provide a service, or which service to provide, the agency has regard to the assessed needs for adoption support services, listens to the service user's wishes and feelings and considers their welfare and safety. NMS 15.

....

What can we do if we have trouble handling our child's behaviour?

You could begin by visiting your GP and requesting referral to a consultant child psychologist, psychiatrist or psychotherapist. You could also consult the organisations and services listed in Section 4 as well as those in this section. In addition, local authorities and voluntary adoption agencies provide post-adoption support, but services available from different agencies are variable. Contact your agency to find out what they offer.

Will we be able to have adoption support services from a local authority, even if we adopted several years ago?

Yes. This is described in Section 4. You have a right to an assessment of your adoption support needs. Remember that approaching professionals at a post-adoption/adoption support centre, or adoption or adoption support workers (ASSAs) in your local authority will be important, especially at times of crises, as these professionals will have a good understanding of adoption and therefore could be particularly helpful.

About disruption

"Disruption" is a term commonly used by social workers to describe an adoption (or foster placement) that does not work out.

A placement can disrupt (i.e. break down) for many reasons: for instance, if the child and adoptive parents are unable to bond or attach to each other; if the child has difficulties for which the adoptive parents were not adequately prepared; or if there is not adequate adoption support for the family.

Needless to say, disrupted adoptions bring immense grief, guilt and anger to both the adoptive parents and for the child. Some local authorities and adoption agencies provide a "disruption meeting". This meeting will include the adopters, all involved social workers, the current carers for the child, possibly the birth parents. It is independently chaired. It considers the adoptive parents' histories up to the match, how the match came to be made and what happened during the placement and how it ended. The aim is to inform ongoing work with and planning for the child and to help everyone involved to reflect on, understand and learn from what happened.

Department of Health Publications
www.gov.uk/government/publications

Depression Alliance
Promotes greater understanding of depression to reduce the stigma associated with it. Produces a free booklet, 'The Young Person's Guide to Stress'.

20 Great Dover Street
London SE1 4LX
Tel: 0845 123 2320
email: information@depressionalliance.org
www.depressionalliance.org

DORE
Provides assessment, consultation and treatment for children, adolescents and adults who may have dyslexia, dyspraxia or attention difficulties. Contact the Centre for further information about its services and its fees.

7 Clarendon Place
Leamington Spa CV32 5QL
Tel: 0333 123 0100
email: info@dore.co.uk
www.dore.co.uk

Faith in Families (formerly Catholic Children's Society (Nottingham))
7 Colwick Road, West Bridgford
Nottingham NG2 5FR
Tel: 0115 955 8811
email: enquiries@faithinfamilies.org
www.faithinfamilies.org

Family and Childcare Trust (formerly Family and Parenting Institute)
Supports parents and offers practical help in bringing up children and promotes the well-being of families. Services include publications and conferences.

The Bridge, 81 Southwark Bridge Road
London SE1 0NQ
Tel: 020 7940 7510
email: info@familyandchildcaretrust.org
www.familyandchildcaretrust.org

Family Futures Consortium Ltd
An adoption and adoption support agency, which specialises in therapeutic work for children who have experienced early trauma and who have attachment difficulties.

3 & 4 Floral Place
7–9 Northampton Grove
London N1 2PL
Tel: 020 7354 4161 (Parent advice line)
email: contact@familyfutures.co.uk
www.familyfutures.co.uk

Family Rights Group (FRG)
A national organisation that advises families who are in contact with social services, about the care of their children.

The Print House, 18 Ashwin Street
London E8 3DL
Tel: 0808 801 0366 (Advice line)
email: advice@frg.org.uk
www.frg.org.uk

First4Adoption
A dedicated information service for people interested in adopting a child from England. Information line: 10am–6pm Monday–Friday
Tel: 0300 222 0022
email: helpdesk@first4adoption.org.uk
www.first4adoption.org.uk

Fostering Network
Provides support and information for foster carers to ensure that all children who are fostered receive the highest standards of care.

87 Blackfriars Road, London SE1 8HA
Tel: 020 7620 6400
email: info@fostering.net
www.fostering.net

Scotland office
2nd Floor, Ingram House
227 Ingram Street, Glasgow G1 1DA
Tel: 0141 204 1400
email: scotland@fostering.net
www.fostering.net

Wales office
1 Caspian Point
Pierhead Street
Cardiff Bay
Cardiff CF10 4DQ
Tel: 029 2044 0940
email: wales@fostering.net

Northern Ireland
40 Montgomery Road
Belfast BT6 9HL
Tel: 028 9070 5056
email: ni@fostering.net

General Register Office for Northern Ireland
Oxford House
49–55 Chichester Street
Belfast BT1 4HL
Tel: 028 9151 3101
www.nidirect.gov.uk/gro

Health and Care Professions Council (HCPC) (formerly General Social Care Council (GSCC))
Regulatory body for the social care profession in England.

Park House
184 Kennington Park Road
London SE11 4BU
Tel: 0845 300 6184
www.hcpc-uk.org

Home Education Advisory Service (HEAS)
A UK-based national charity providing information and support for home education. Produces information, provides support for parents, works with LEAs to monitor and inspect home education programmes.

PO Box 98, Welwyn Garden City
Hertfordshire AL8 6AN
Tel: 01707 371 854
email: enquiries@heas.org.uk
www.heas.org.uk

Independent Panel for Special Education Advice (IPSEA)
A charity that aims to ensure that children with special educational needs receive the special education provision to which they are legally entitled. Provides free, independent advice; free advice on appealing to the Special Educational Needs Tribunal (including representation, if needed); second opinions from professionals.

Hunters Court
Debden Road
Saffron Walden CB11 4AA
Advice line: 0800 018 4016
Tribunal appeals only: 0845 602 9579
www.ipsea.org.uk

Independent Review Mechanism (IRM)
Reviews adoption and fostering suitability applications from prospective and current carers whose agency has decided not to approve them. Run by BAAF for the Department for Education.

Unit 4, Pavilion Business Park
Royds Hall Road
Wortley
Leeds LS12 6AJ
Tel: 0845 450 3956
www.independentreviewmechanism.org.uk

Independent Review Mechanism (IRM) Cymru
7 Cleeve House
Lambourne Crescent
Cardiff CF14 5GP
Tel: 0845 873 1305
www.irmcymru.org.uk

The Institute for Arts in Therapy and Education
A college of higher education dedicated to in-depth theoretical and practical study of artistic, imaginative and emotional expression and understanding and enhancement of emotional well-being.

2–18 Britannia Row, London N1 8PA
Tel: 020 7704 2534
email: info@artspsychotherapy.org
www.artspsychotherapy.org

provides advice to LEAs and offers specialist services, such as enuresis (bedwetting) clinics, audiology services, and support/ advice for families and children with physical and emotional difficulties. Contact your local authority or LEA to find phone numbers for your local School Health Teams.

Scottish Health on the Web (SHOW)
Provided by the NHS in Scotland, this site provides general health information, contact details of all NHS Trusts, and links to other websites.

www.show.scot.nhs.uk

Social, Emotional and Behavioural Difficulties Association (SEBDA)
Promotes services for children and young people who have emotional and behavioural difficulties, and supports professionals working with young people. Produces journal, *Emotional and Behavioural Difficulties*, that provides a variety of articles written mainly by professionals in the field. The journal is available from SAGE Publications.

SEBDA
c/o Goldwyn School
Godinton Lane, Great Chart
Ashford, Kent TN23 3BT
email: admin@sebda.org
www.sebda.org

Special Education Consortium
See contact details for Council for Disabled Children.

The Stationery Office
Tel: 0870 242 2345
www.tsoshop.co.uk (online shop)

TalkAdoption
A free, confidential national helpline for young people (to 25 years old) who have a link with adoption, whether adoptee, friend or relative.

Tuesday–Friday 3–9 pm
Tel: 0808 808 1234
www.afteradoption.org.uk

The Who Cares? Trust
Promotes services for children and young people in public care and those who have left public care. Publishes 'Who Cares?' magazine quarterly.

Kemp House
152–160 City Road
London EC1V 2NP
Tel: 020 7251 3117
email: mailbox@thewhocarestrust.org.uk
www.thewhocarestrust.org.uk

UK Youth
A network of organisations dedicated to supporting young people to realise their potential. Delivers and supports high-quality voluntary work and informal education for young people. Provides publications for young people and youth workers about emotional/ behavioural issues.

7 Heron Quays
Canary Wharf
London E14 4JB
Tel: 020 3137 3810
email: info@ukyouth.org
www.ukyouth.org

United Kingdom Council for Psychotherapy (UKCP)
Holds national register of psychotherapists and gives details of local psychotherapists and counsellors.

2nd Floor, Edward House
2 Wakley Street
London EC1V 7LT
Tel: 020 7014 9955
email:info@ukcp.org.uk
www.psychotherapy.org.uk

YoungMinds: the children's mental health charity
The national charity committed to improving the mental health of all children and young people. Produces a variety of information about many mental health issues, including 'YoungMinds Magazine'. Provides a consultancy service; works with health, education and social services, and

the voluntary sector to develop services for children with mental health problems.

Suite 11, Baden Place
Crosby Row
London SE1 1YW
Tel: 020 7089 5050
www.youngminds.org.uk

YoungMinds Parents' Information Service

A telephone service providing information and advice for anyone with concerns about the mental health of a child or young person.

Helpline: 0808 802 5544
www.youngminds.org.uk/for_parents

Youth Access

The largest provider of free and confidential youth counselling and information centres throughout the UK. You can find your local service on:
www.youthaccess.org.uk

Appendix 3:
National Minimum Standards (NMS) applicable to the provision of adoption services

General Introduction

The National Minimum Standards (NMS) together with the adoption regulations form the basis of the regulatory framework under the Care Standards Act 2000 for the conduct of adoption agencies and adoption support agencies.

The values statement below explains the important principles which underpin these Standards.

Values – children

- The child's welfare, safety and needs are at the centre of the adoption process.

- Adopted children should have an enjoyable childhood, and benefit from excellent parenting and education, enjoying a wide range of opportunities to develop their talents and skills leading to a successful adult life.

- Children are entitled to grow up as part of a loving family that can meet their developmental needs during childhood and beyond.

- Children's wishes and feelings are important and will be actively sought and fully taken into account at all stages of the adoption process.

- Delays should be avoided as they can have a severe impact on the health and development of the children waiting to be adopted.

- A sense of identity is important to a child's well-being. To help children develop this, their ethnic origin, cultural background, religion, language and sexuality need to be properly recognised and positively valued and promoted.

- The particular needs of disabled children and children with complex needs will be fully recognised and taken into account.

- Where a child cannot be cared for in a suitable manner in their own country, intercountry adoption may be considered as an alternative means of providing a permanent family.

- Children, birth parents/guardians and families and adoptive parents and families will be valued and respected.

- A genuine partnership between all those involved in adoption is essential for the NMS to deliver the best outcomes for children; this includes the Government, local government, other statutory agencies, Voluntary Adoption Agencies and Adoption Support Agencies.

Values – adopted adults and birth relatives

- Adoption is an evolving life-long process for all those involved – adopted adults, and birth and adoptive relatives. The fundamental issues raised by adoption may reverberate and resurface at different times and stages throughout an individual's life.

- Adopted people should have access to information and services to enable them to address adoption-related matters throughout their life.

- Agencies have a duty to provide services that considers the welfare of all parties involved and should consider the implications of decisions and actions for everyone involved.

- Agencies should seek to work in partnership with all parties involved, taking account of their views and wishes in decision-making.

- Agencies should acknowledge differences in people's circumstances and establish policies that provide non-discriminatory services.

- Adopted adults have their adoptive identity safeguarded and the right to decide whether to be involved in contact or communication with birth family members.

The detailed standards are the basis for expected outcomes. These outcomes include the following:

- Children know that their views, wishes and feelings are taken into account in all aspects of their care; are helped to understand why it may not be possible to act upon their wishes in all cases; and know how to obtain support and make a complaint.

- Children have a positive self view, emotional resilience and knowledge and understanding of their background.

- Children enjoy sound relationships with their prospective adopters, interact positively with others and behave appropriately.

- Children feel safe and are safe; children understand how to protect themselves and are protected from significant harm including neglect, abuse and accident.

- Children live in a healthy environment where their physical, emotional and psychological health is promoted and where they are able to access the services they need to meet their health needs.

- Children are able to enjoy their interests, develop confidence in their skills and are supported and encouraged to engage in leisure activities.

- The education and achievements of children is actively promoted as valuable in itself and as part of their preparation for adulthood. Children are supported to achieve their educational potential.

- Contact with birth parents, siblings, other members of the birth family and significant others is arranged and maintained when it is beneficial to the child.

- Children live with prospective adopters whose home provides adequate space to a suitable standard. The child enjoys access to a range of activities which promote their development.

- The adoption agency approves adopters who can meet most of the needs of looked after children who are to be placed for adoption and who can provide them with a home where the child will feel loved, safe and secure.

- Children have clear and appropriate information about themselves, their birth parents and families, and life before their adoption.

- Birth parents and birth families take an active part in the planning and implementation of their child's adoption.

- Children benefit from stable placements and are matched and placed with prospective adopters who can meet most, if not all, of their assessed needs.

- Children feel loved, safe and secure with their prospective adoptive parents with whom they were originally placed; and these children were placed within 12 months of the decision of the agency's decision-maker that they should be placed for adoption.

- Children and adults affected by adoption receive an assessment of their adoption support needs.

- Service users confirm that the adoption support services provided met or are meeting their assessed needs.

- Adopted adults and birth relatives are assisted to obtain information in relation to the adoption, where appropriate, and contact is facilitated between an adopted adult and their birth relative if that is what both parties want.

- The adoption panel and decision-maker make timely, quality and appropriate recommendations/decisions in line with the overriding objective to promote the welfare of children throughout their lives.

Where there are changes, these are noted under the headings in *Effective Panels* with page references. There is a section in the introduction to the Guidance – para 5, 'Making the adoption process work well' – which is included here, in summary.

Reproduced from *Adoption: National Minimum Standards*, Department for Education, 2011.
This information is licensed under the terms of the Open Government Licence
(www.education.gov.uk/publications/eOrderingDownload/Adoption–NMS.pdf
accessed 14/11/2011)

Appendix 4:
The Adopters' Charter

The Adopters' Charter was introduced by the Department for Education in November 2011. Its Ministerial Foreword expresses the hope that adoption agencies 'will endorse, implement and build on its principles and that, at the same time, it will give adopters the confidence to question agency planning and decision making'. The Charter is reproduced below.

Children come first

- Adoption is first and foremost a service for children who cannot live with their birth family. Children should be helped to understand what adoption means and supported throughout the adoption journey and beyond.

- Adoption is a life-changing decision that affects the child, and his or her birth and adoptive families. It must be made with the child's best interests, wishes, feelings and needs at its heart and on the basis of sound evidence and high quality assessments.

Adoption agencies must:

- Ensure that children are placed, with siblings wherever possible, within a timescale that is best for them and without unnecessary delay.

- Treat prospective adopters and adopters with openness, fairness and respect.

- Make prospective adopters' first points of contact informative and welcoming.

- Approach adopter recruitment in the spirit of inclusiveness with a view to identifying potential and opportunity – no-one should be automatically excluded.

- Recruit prospective adopters who can meet all or most of the needs of children waiting for, or likely to need, adoption and signpost prospective adopters to other agencies if there is insufficient local demand.

- Explain to prospective adopters the needs and profiles of the children waiting to be adopted.

- Ensure preparation and training, the home study assessment, and approval process are explained and proceed efficiently.

- Regularly review progress on matching with prospective adopters, and inform them about the Adoption Register and refer them to this within required timescales.

- Provide adopters and prospective adopters with information, counselling and support, as and when needed, throughout the adoption journey and beyond.

- Provide prospective adopters with information about the Independent Review Mechanism.

- Work in partnership, and with other agencies and the Courts, to ensure that all decisions are timely and joined-up.

Adoptive parents must:

- Be aware that adoption often brings challenges as well as joy, be realistic about the needs of children awaiting adoption, and accept that with support they may be able to consider adopting a child with a different profile to the child they originally envisaged adopting.

- Make the most of opportunities to develop their parenting skills, and seek support when needed at the earliest stage.

- Do all they can to enable their adopted child to feel loved and secure, and to reach their potential.

Reproduced from *The Adopter's Charter*, Department for Education, 2011. This information is licensed under the terms of the Open Government Licence (www.dfe.gov.uk/childrenandyoungpeople/families/adoption, accessed 14/11/11).

Appendix 5:
The Adoption Passport

The adoption passport: a support guide for adopters

Children adopted from care can have ongoing needs, and you and your child may benefit from support. This is the support adopters in England may be entitled to:

For your child...

Children adopted from care have priority access to schools, which means that your child should be able to attend whichever school you think best meets their needs (www.gov.uk/schools-admissions). From September 2014, they will also be entitled to free early education from the age of two (tinyurl.com/first4early).

If your child needs extra support, you can ask your local authority to assess their needs for adoption support services (see page 2). If you think your child may have special educational needs you can ask your local authority to assess these needs too.

For you as an adopter...

Many adopters are entitled to adoption leave and pay when their child is placed with them (www.gov.uk/adoption-pay-leave). The law is changing to make this entitlement more similar to maternity and paternity leave pay, and it will include the right to take time off when you are meeting your child, before they move in with you.

Adopters may have priority for council housing (www.gov.uk/council-housing). If you are living in council housing and claiming Housing Benefit or Universal Credit while waiting for a child to move in you can also apply for funding (Discretionary Housing Payments) so that you are not penalised financially while you have an empty spare room.

You are also entitled to a summary of your child's health from his or her local authority's medical adviser before he or she is placed with you, and to a life-story book to help your child understand his or her early life.

Adoption Support Services

Local authorities provide and fund a range of support services for children adopted from care. These support services can include:

- counselling, information and advice
- help with behavioural, attachment and other problems
- money e.g. to help with special care needs, or for former foster parents
- help with contact between an adopted child and his or her birth family
- meetings and events to enable groups of adopters and adoptive children to get together
- training to help adopters to meet the needs of their adoptive child
- short breaks for an adopted child with another carer
- help where an adoption breaks down.

Access to these services depends on your circumstances but you can ask for an assessment *at any time*, no matter how long after the adoption.

Support Services Advice

Your local authority will have an Adoption Support Services Adviser to help you access adoption support and other specialist services, such as Child and Adolescent Mental Health Services. The NHS commissions health services to meet the needs of adopted children, and the National Institute for Health and Care Excellence will produce new guidance so that your GP will understand the problems you may face. The Adoption Support Services Adviser's details should be available on the local authority's website.

Every adopter is entitled to an assessment of their adoption support needs, but local authorities do not have to provide support in response to an assessment. Which services you are able to access will depend on your circumstances. Future changes to the law will mean that local authorities must tell adopters about adoption support services and their right to an assessment, and will give those who receive support a choice about how that support is provided, either by a local authority or through a 'personal budget' to purchase services from a voluntary adoption agency or adoption support agency.

If you want advice on adoption support you can also contact one of the many adoption support organisations, such as Adoption UK (www.adoptionuk.org.uk) or the British Association for Adoption and Fostering (www.baaf.org.uk), or read the e learning materials soon to be on the First4Adoption web-site which will explore the effect of children's experiences on their development and the services available to help them.

Which local authority?

The local authority that places the child with you is responsible for assessing your adoption support needs for three years after the adoption. After three years it becomes the responsibility of the local authority where you live (if different).

Comments and complaints

If you are unhappy with the support provided by your local authority, or with the time taken to carry out an assessment, you can complain under the Local Authority Complaints Procedure. Thereafter if you are not satisfied you may be able to refer your complaint to the Local Government Ombudsman (www.lgo.org.uk). You will also soon be able to raise general concerns with the new Champion for adopters, foster carers and special guardians.

FIRST 4 ADOPTION is the dedicated information service for anyone interested in adopting a child in England. It is managed by Coram Children's Legal Centre, Coram and Adoption UK, and supported and funded by the Department for Education.

- Call First4Adoption: 0300 222 0022
- Visit our website: first4adoption.org.uk
- Follow us on Twitter: @First4Adoption

Supported by

Department for Education

© Crown copyright 2013

Index